ALPHABET COLORING BOOK.

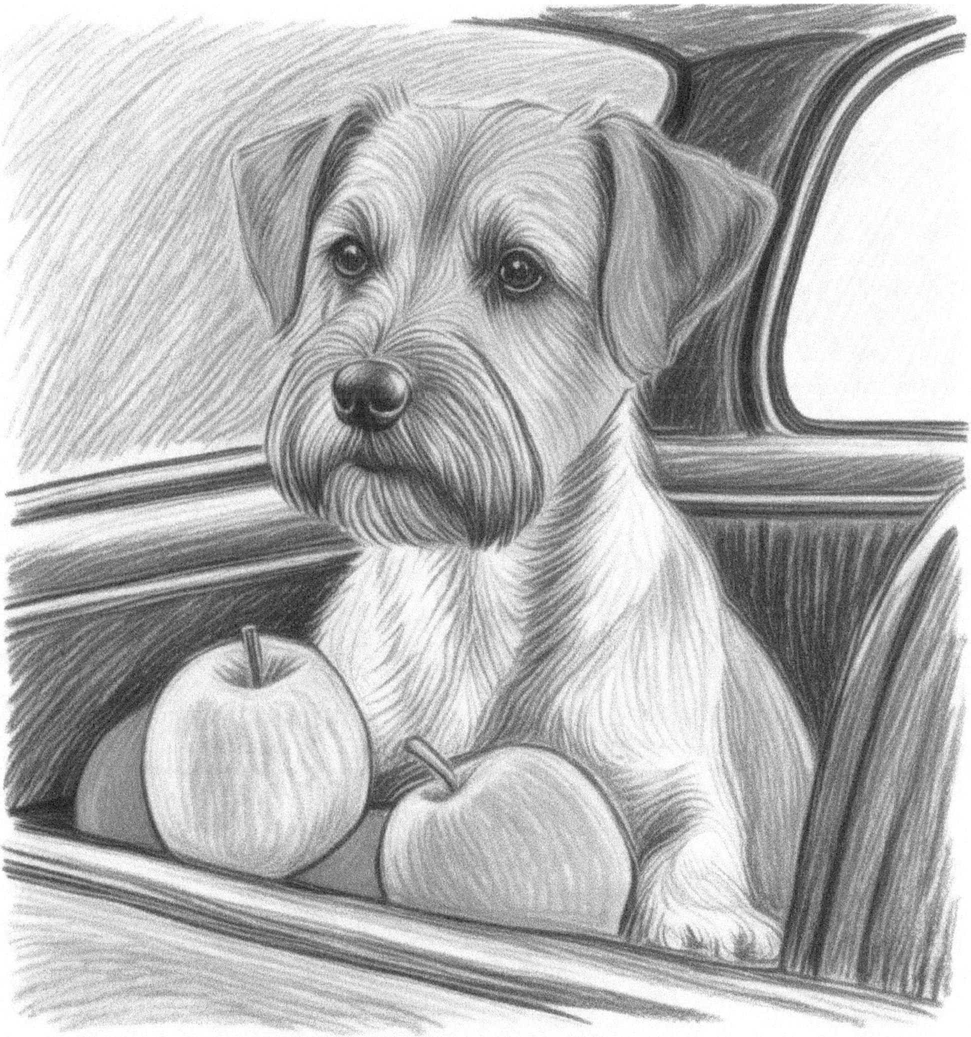

Josner Leal.

First edition: May 2024.

Any form of reproduction and/or transformation of this work without authorization from the intellectual property owners is prohibited, except as provided by law. The infringement of the aforementioned rights may constitute a crime against intellectual property, in accordance with the Copyright and Related Rights law, for which it may be criminally sanctioned.

DRAW EVERY LETTER AND EVERY WORD WITH THE COLORS OF YOUR PREFERENCE, IDENTIFY THE IMAGES AND BRING THEM TO LIFE WITH THE COLORS OF YOUR IMAGINATION.

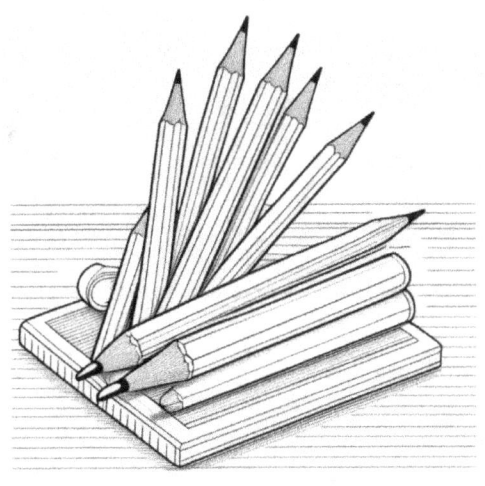

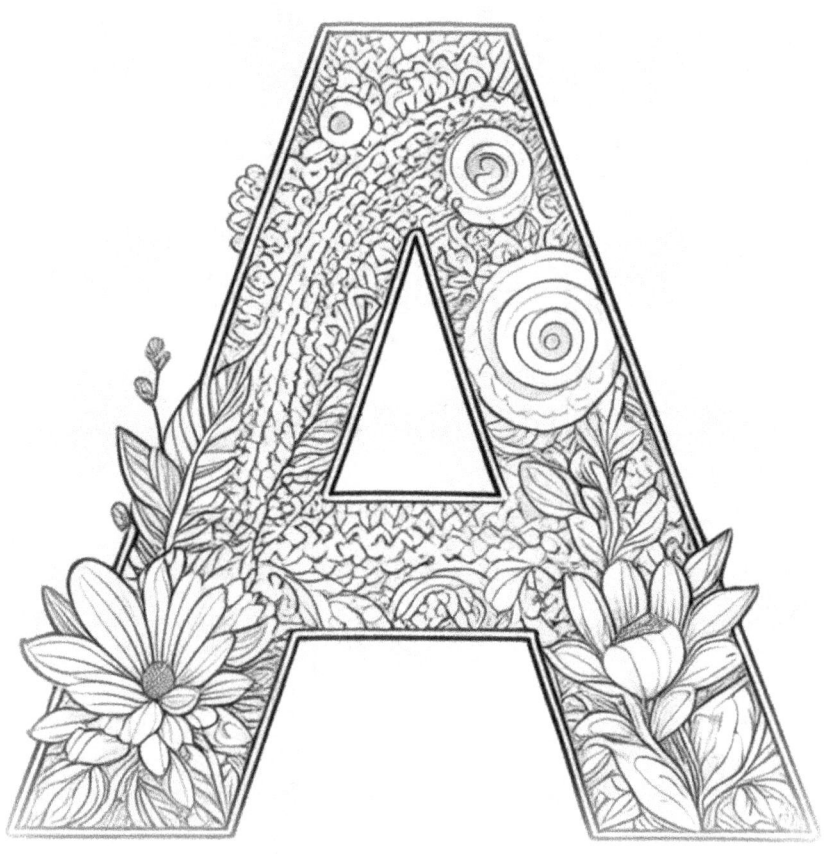

Angelfish

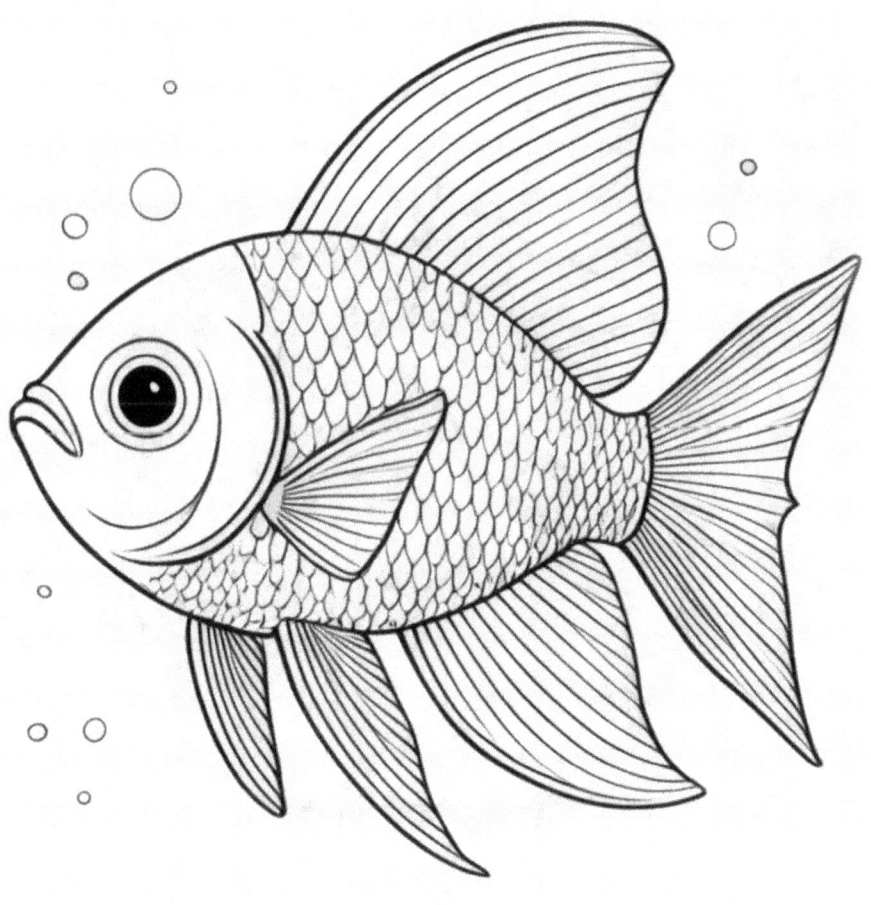

Apple

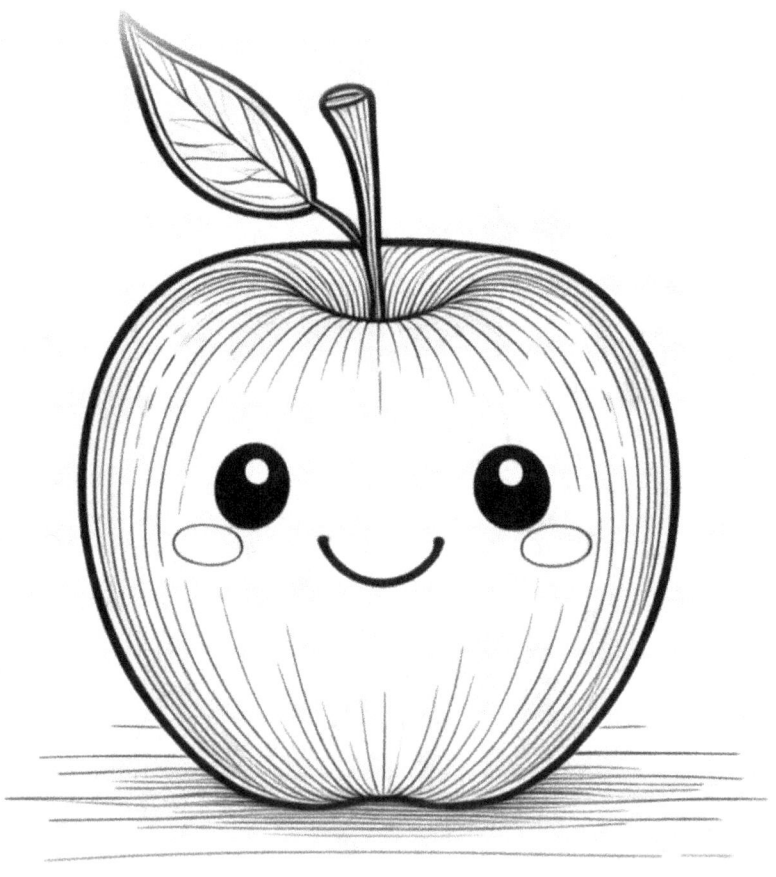

Airplane

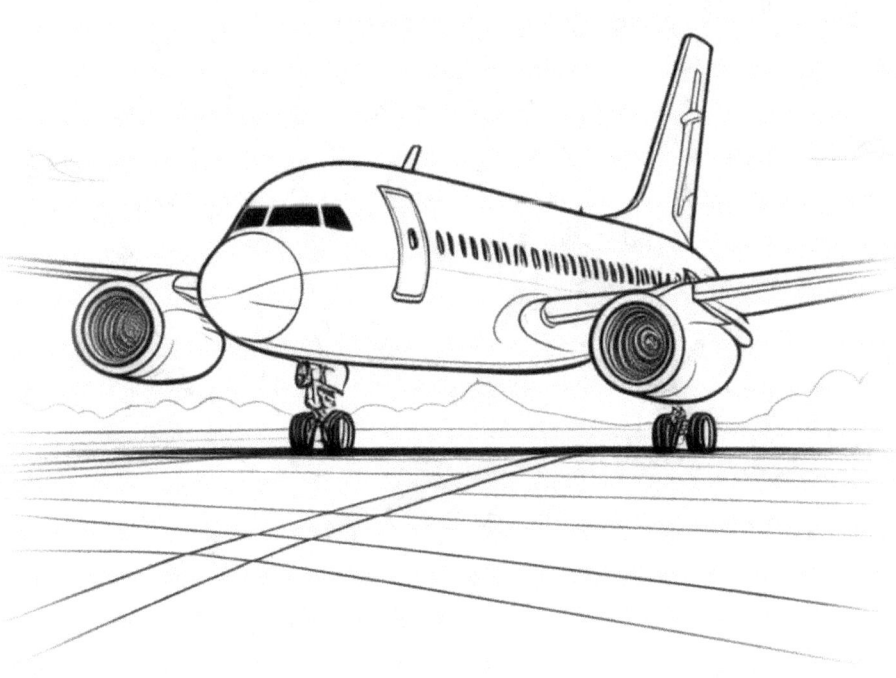

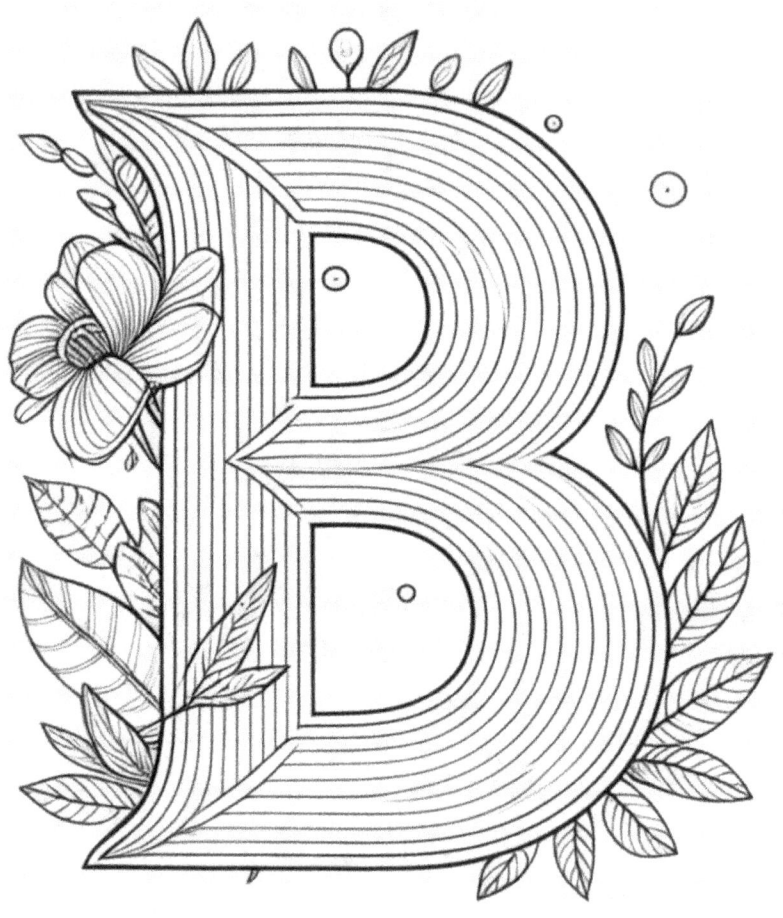

Bear

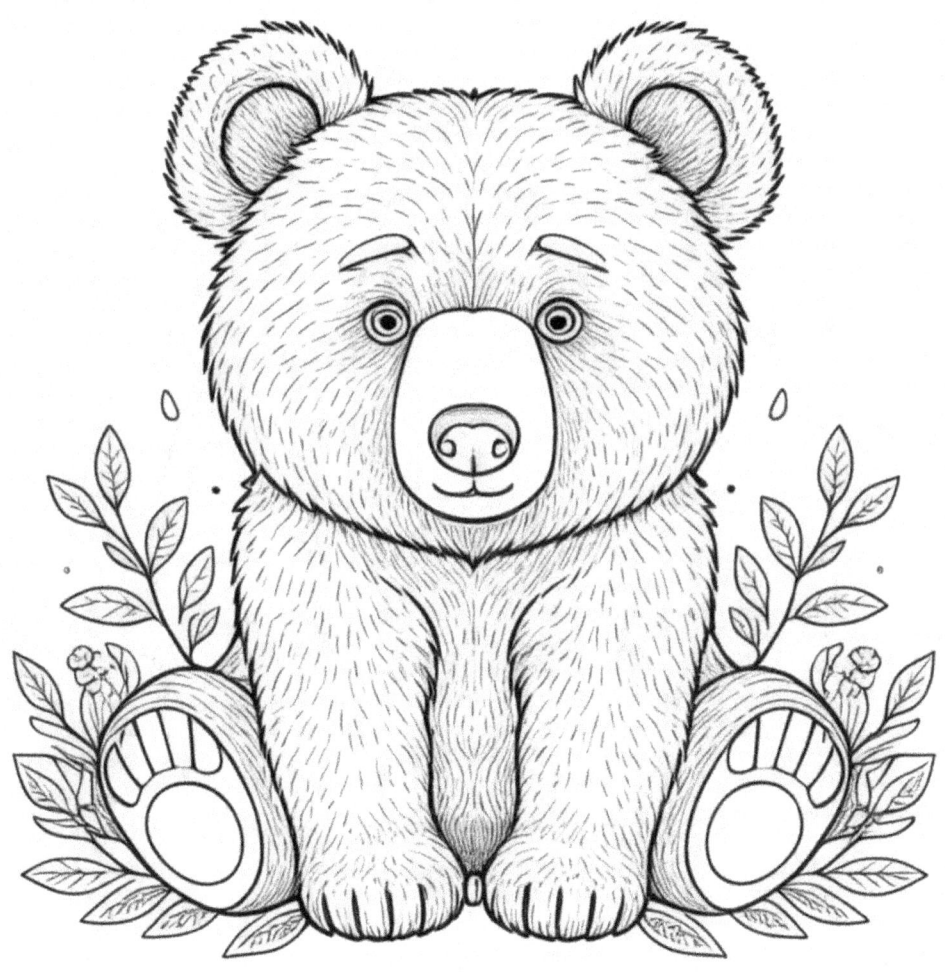

Banana

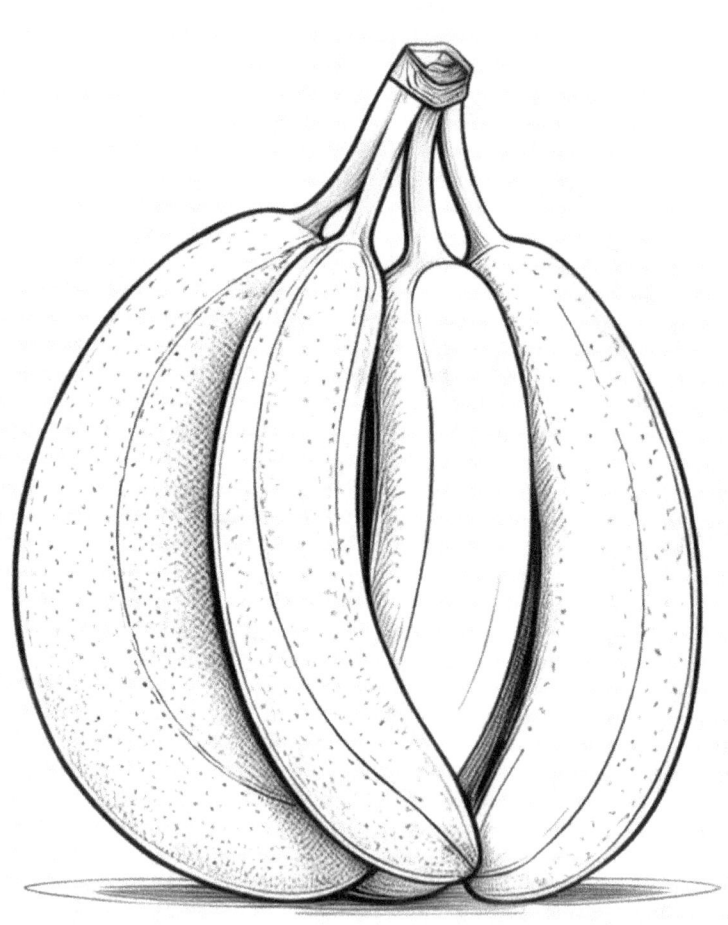

Bicycle

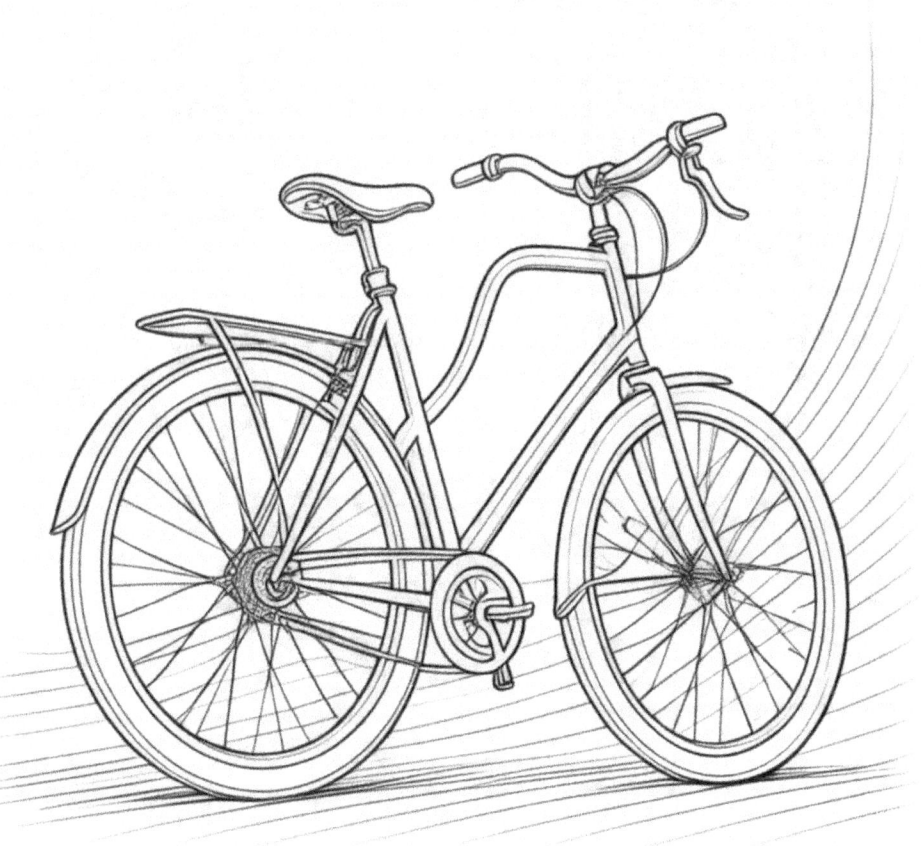

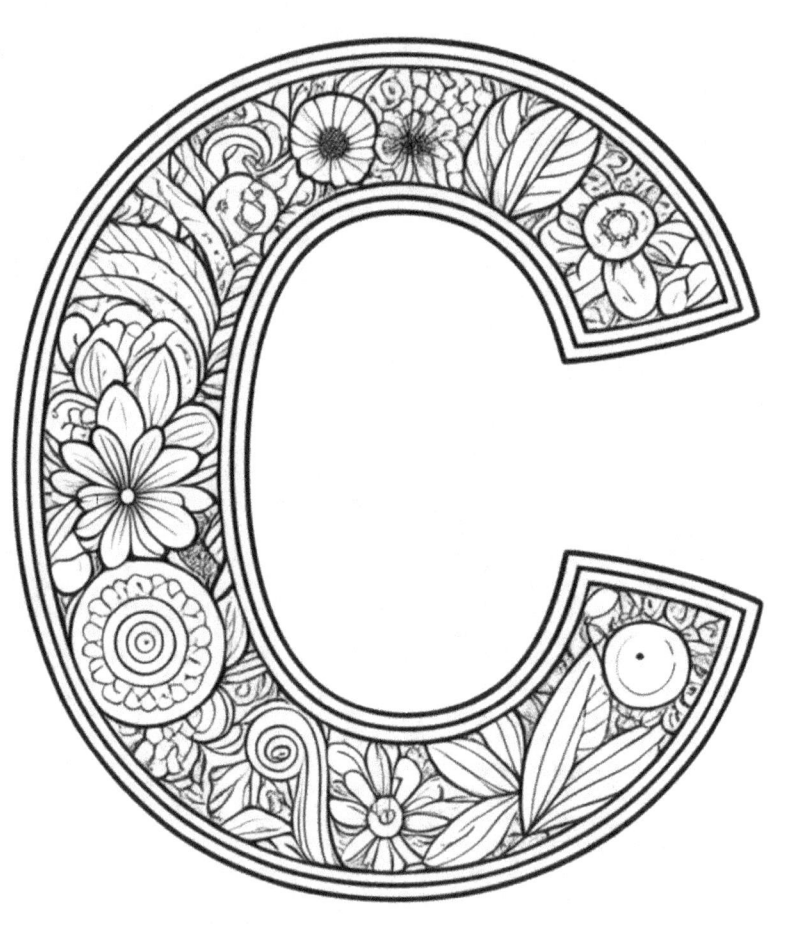

Cat

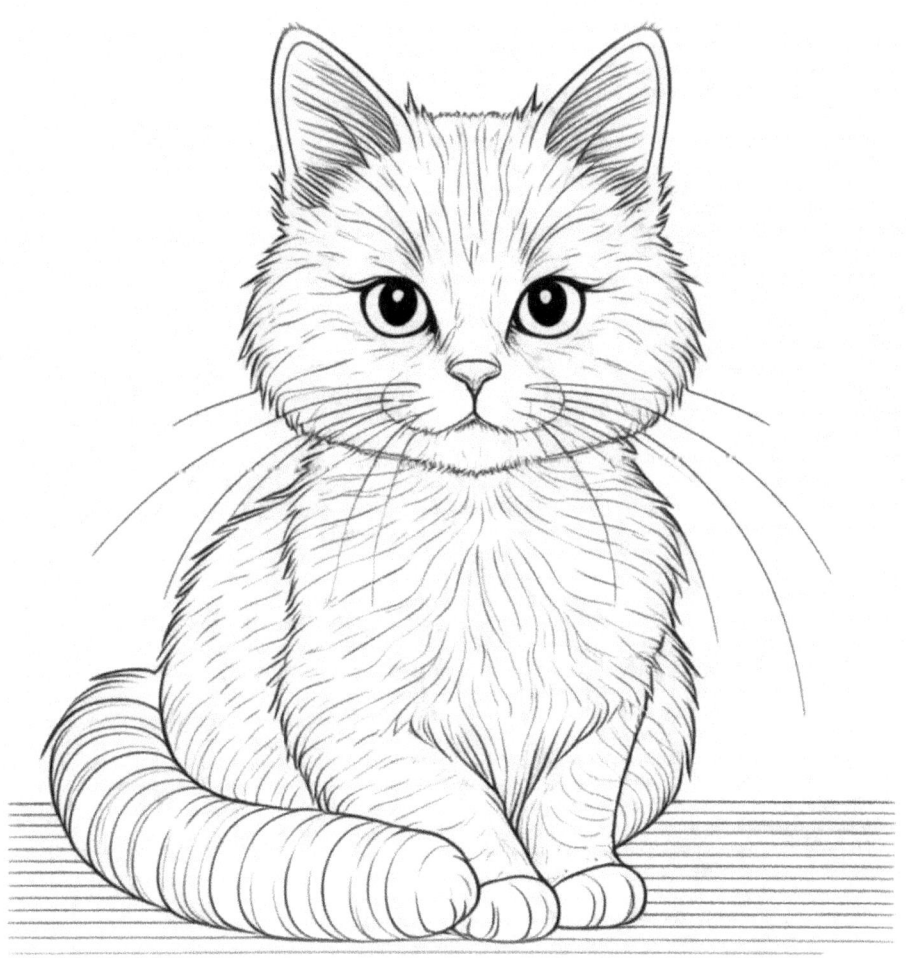

Cherries

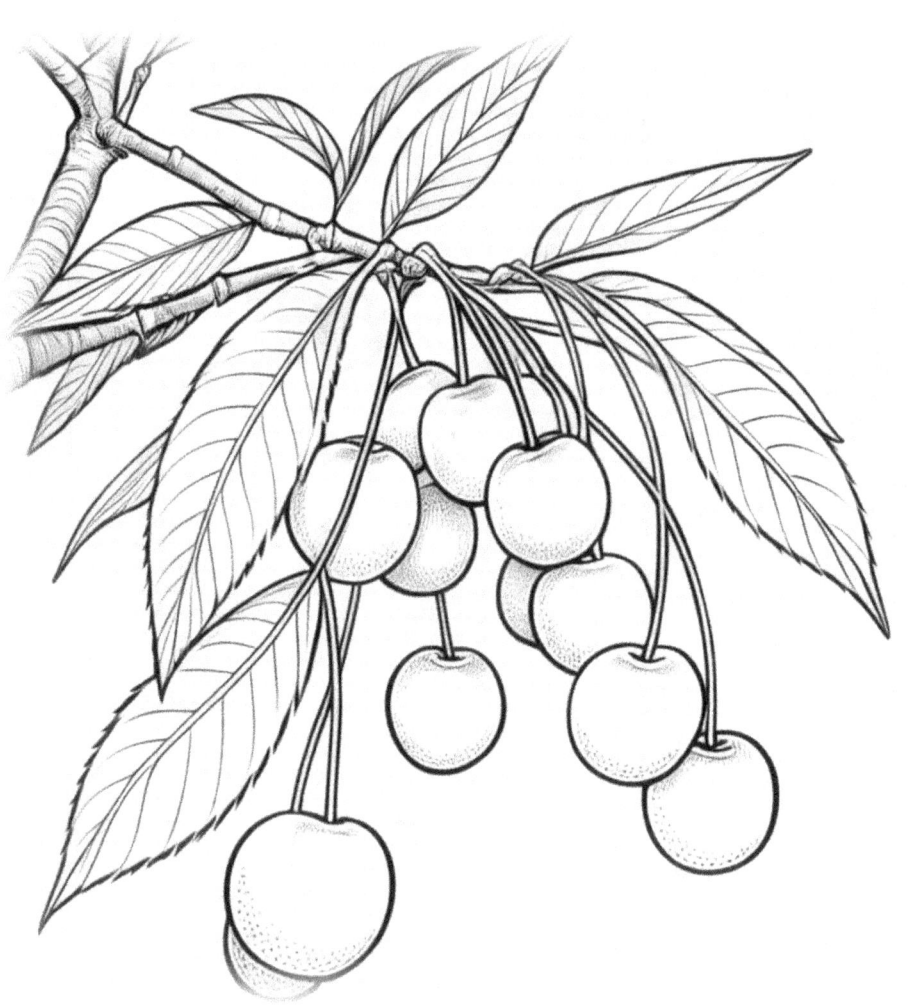

Car

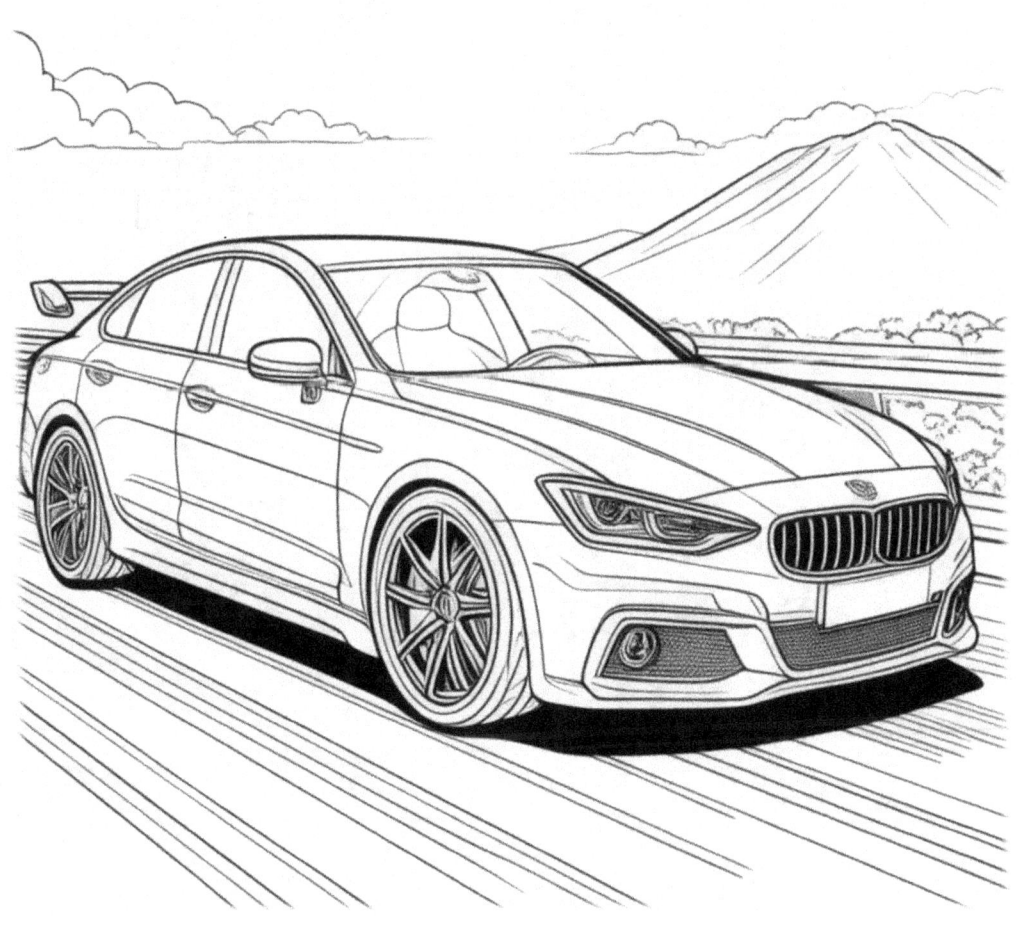

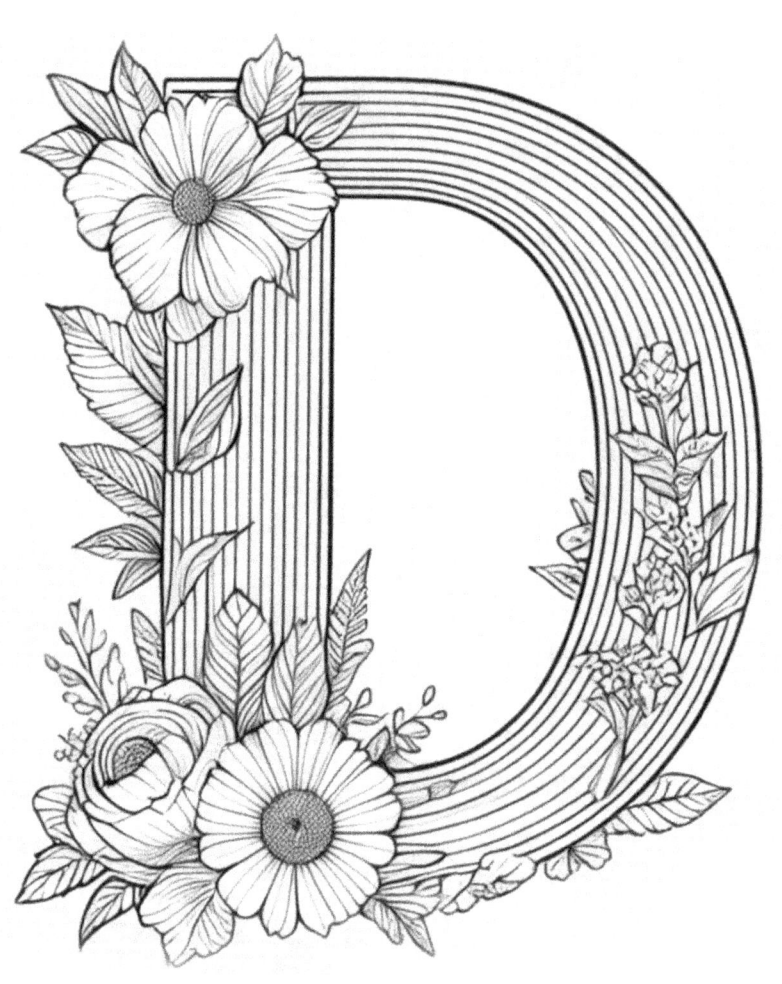

Dog

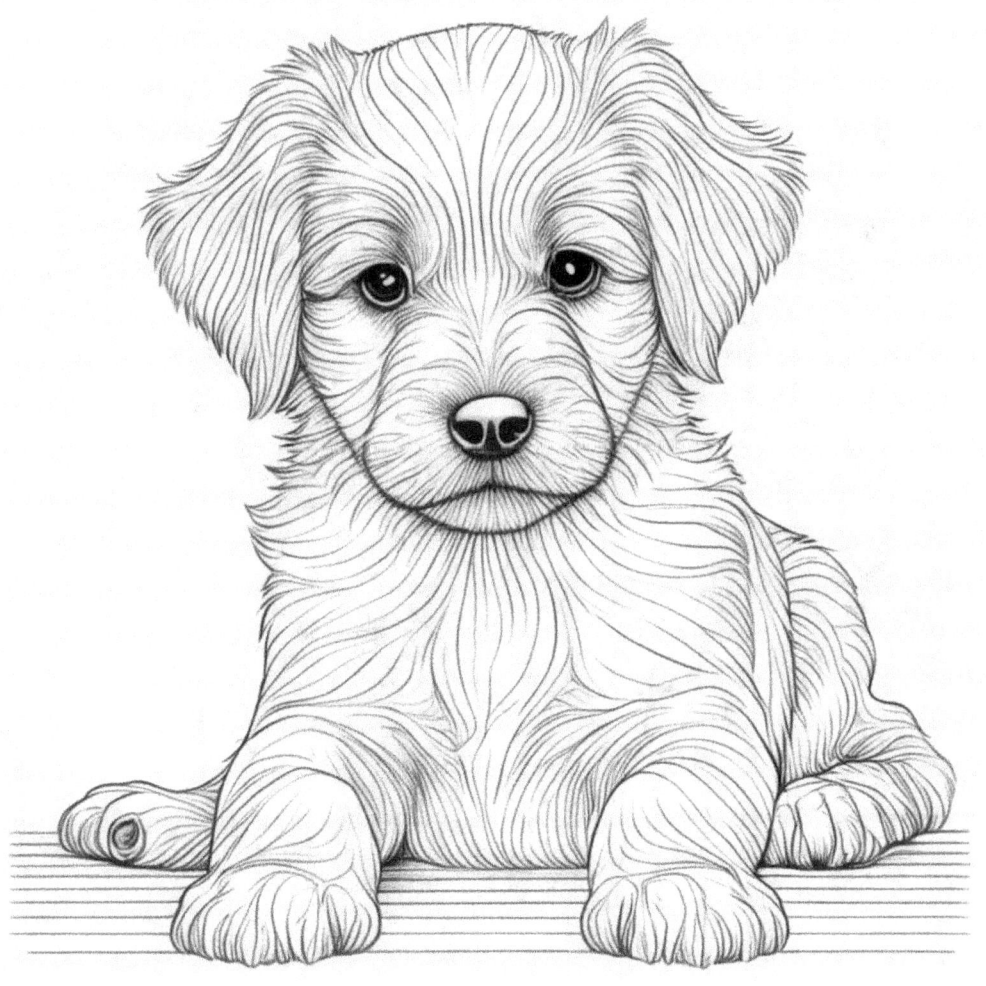

Daisy

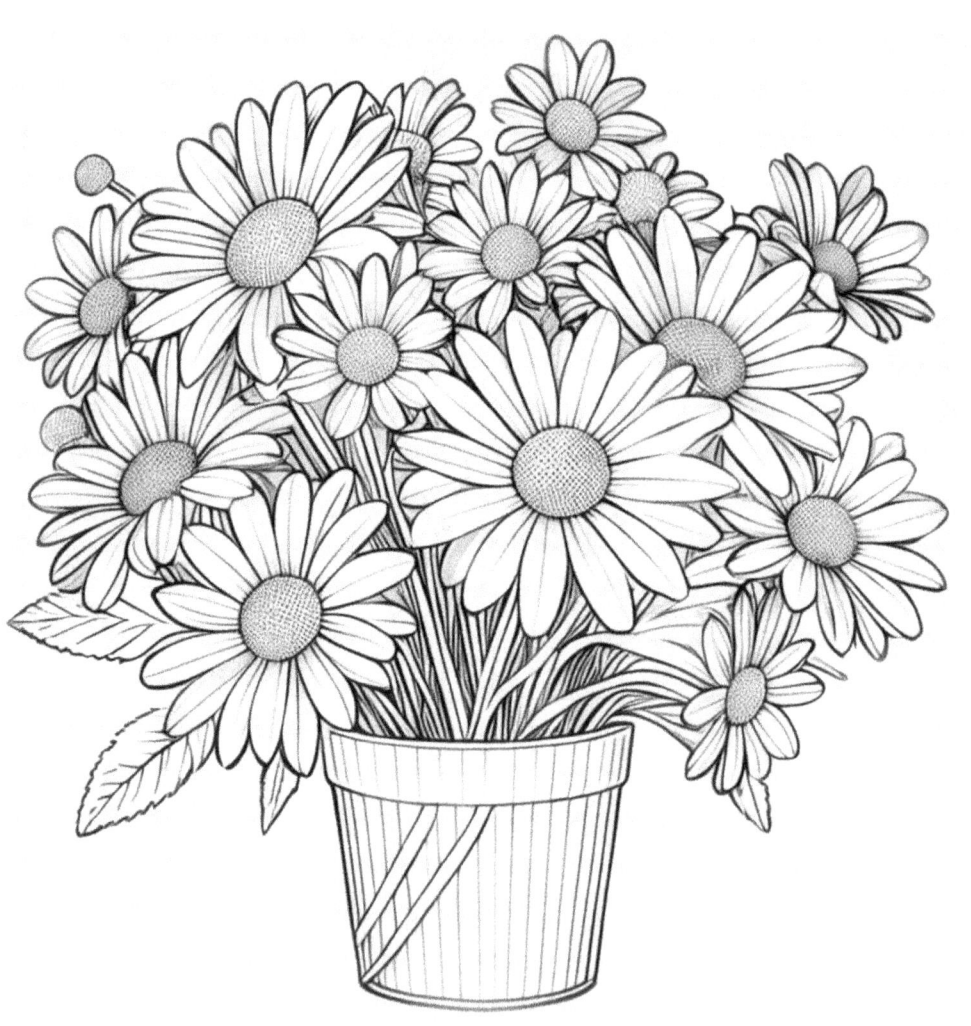

Drone

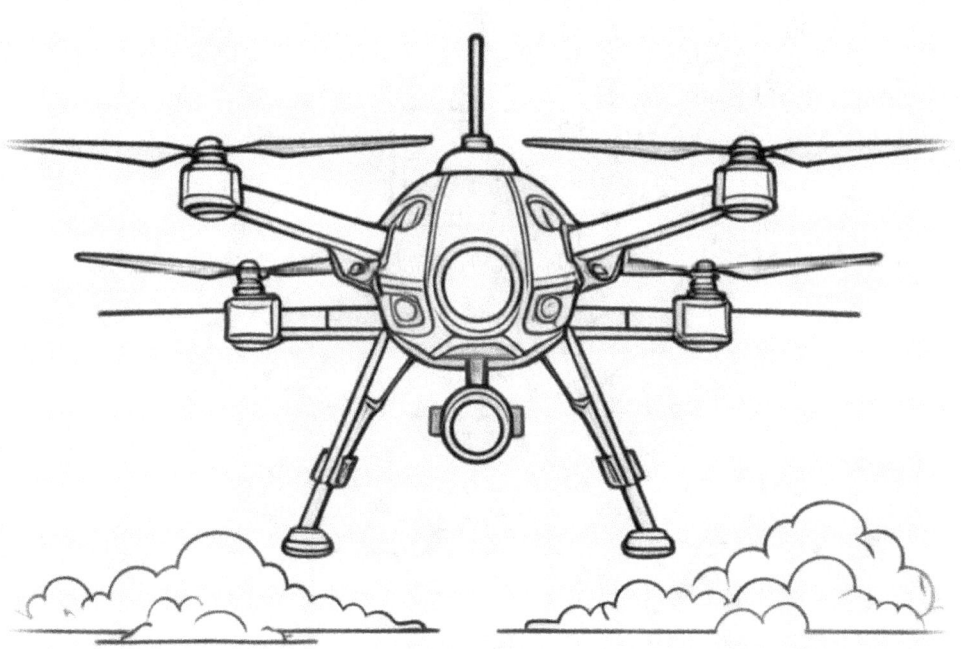

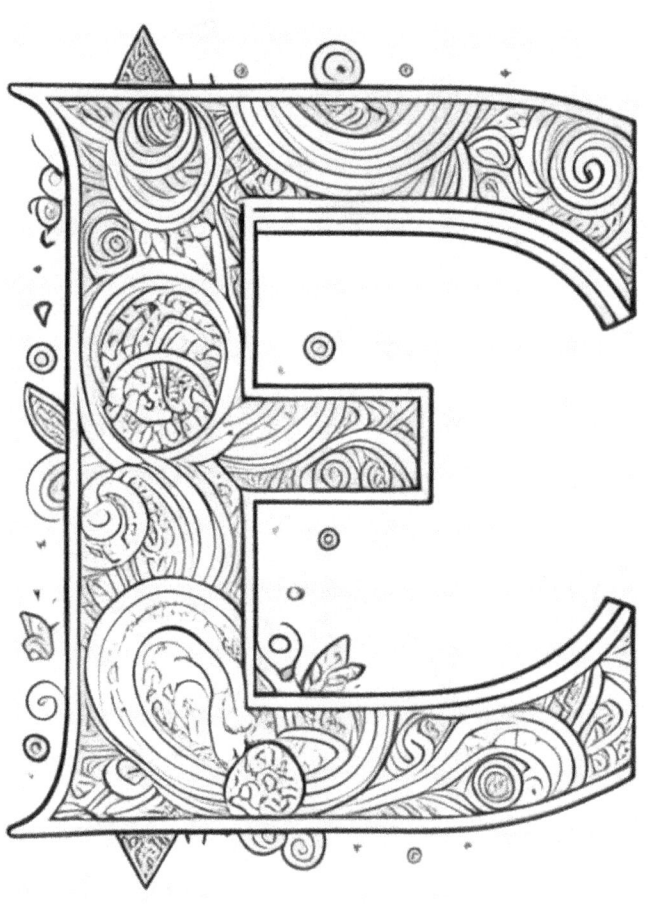

Elephant

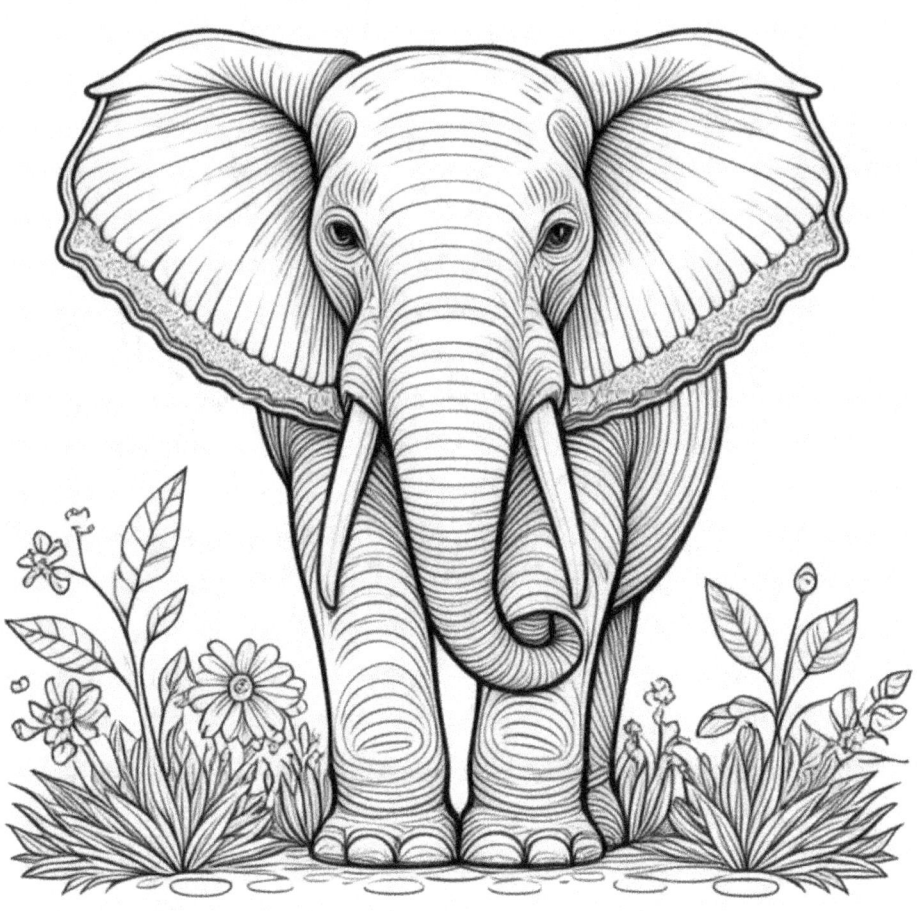

Elderberry

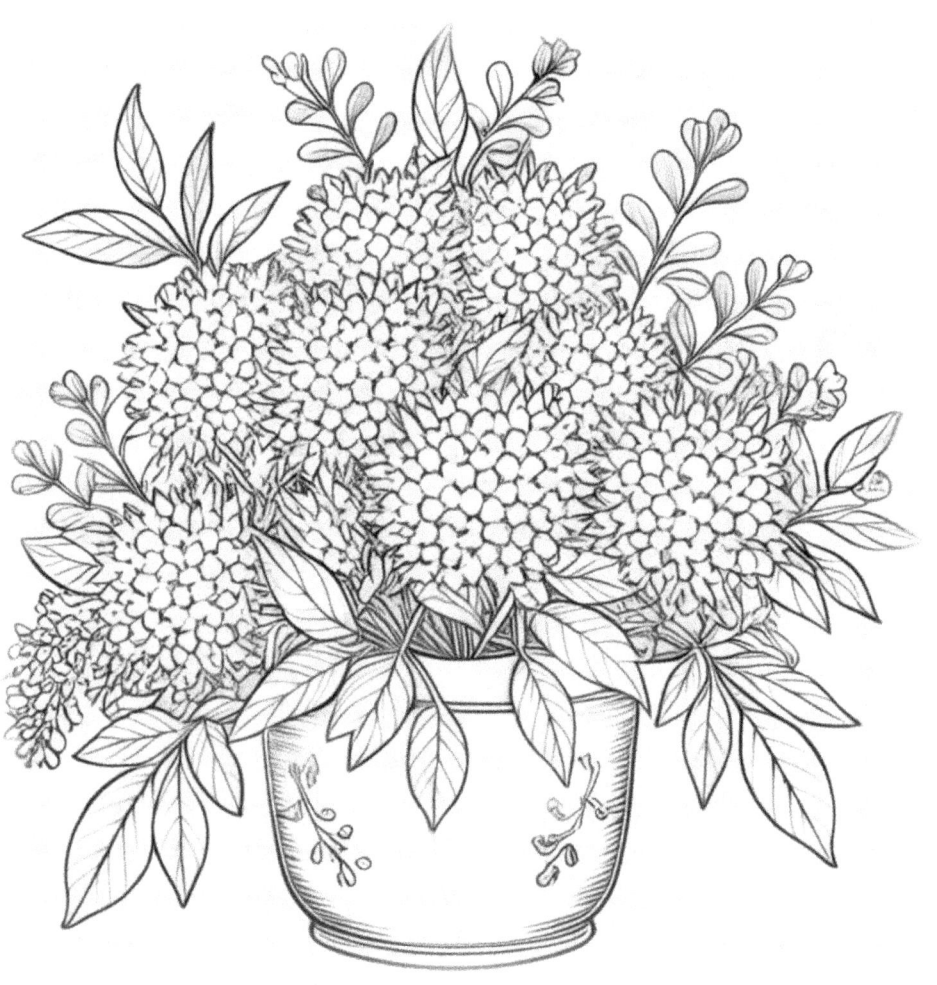

Escalator

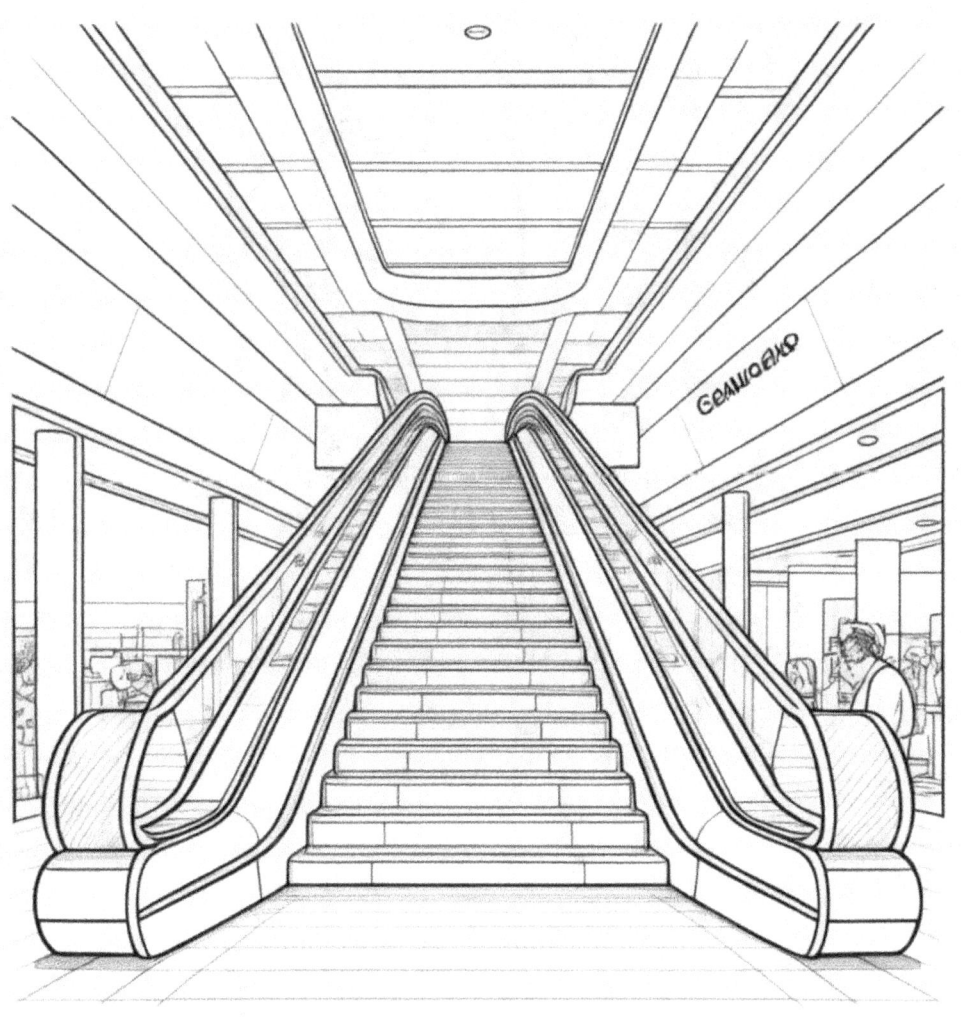

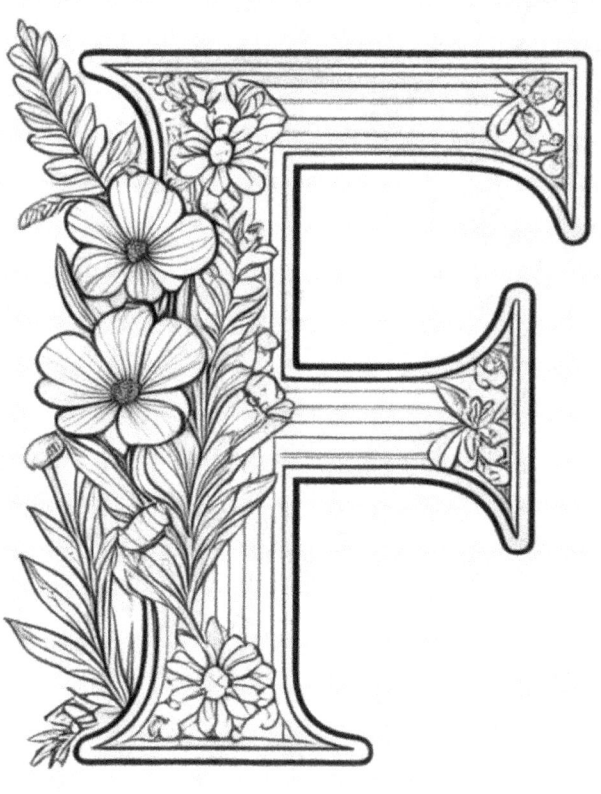

Fox

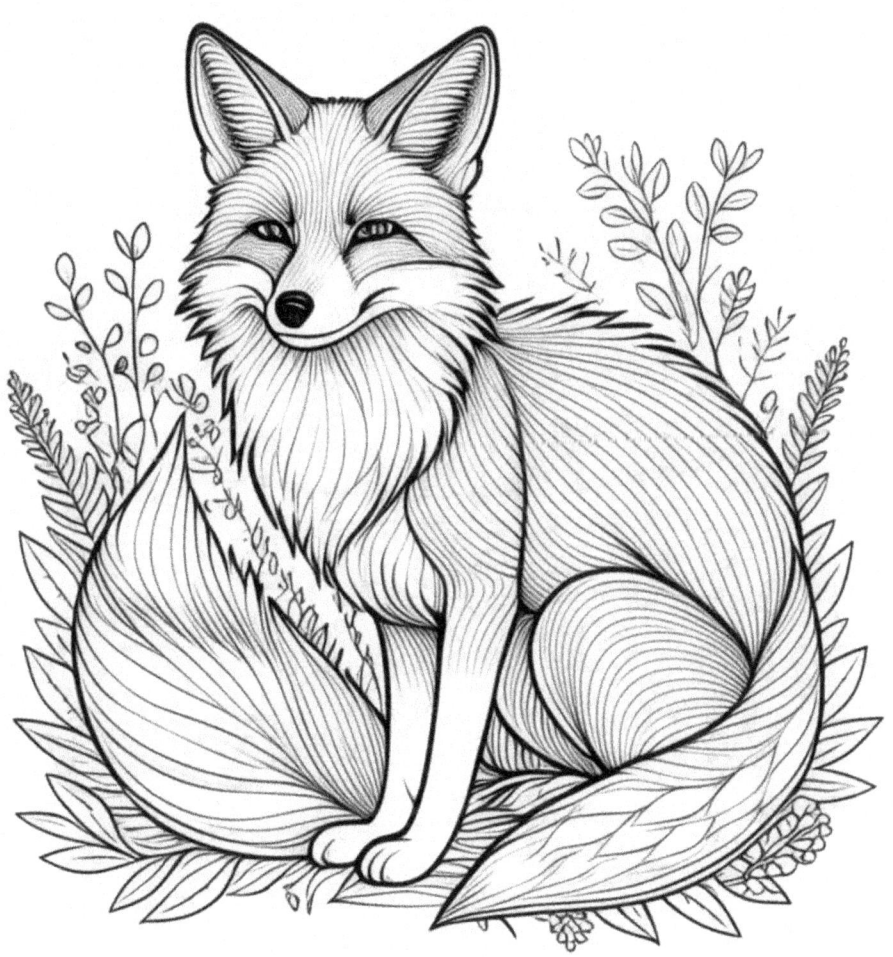

Fig

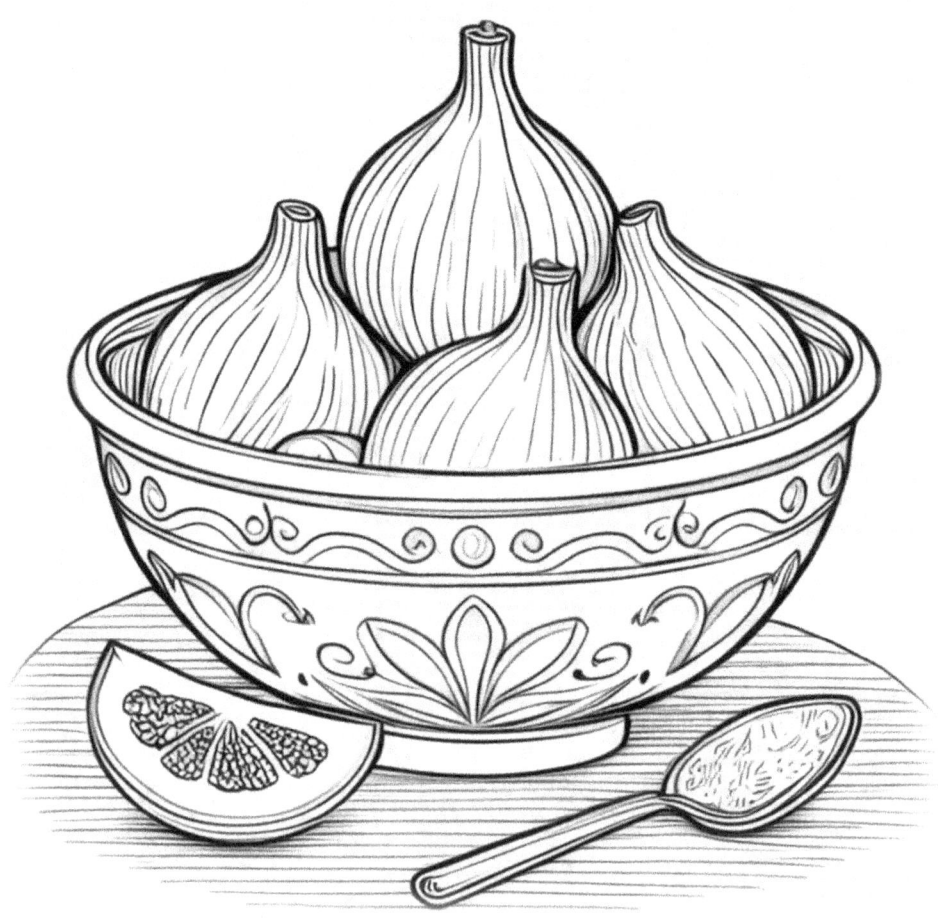

Ferry

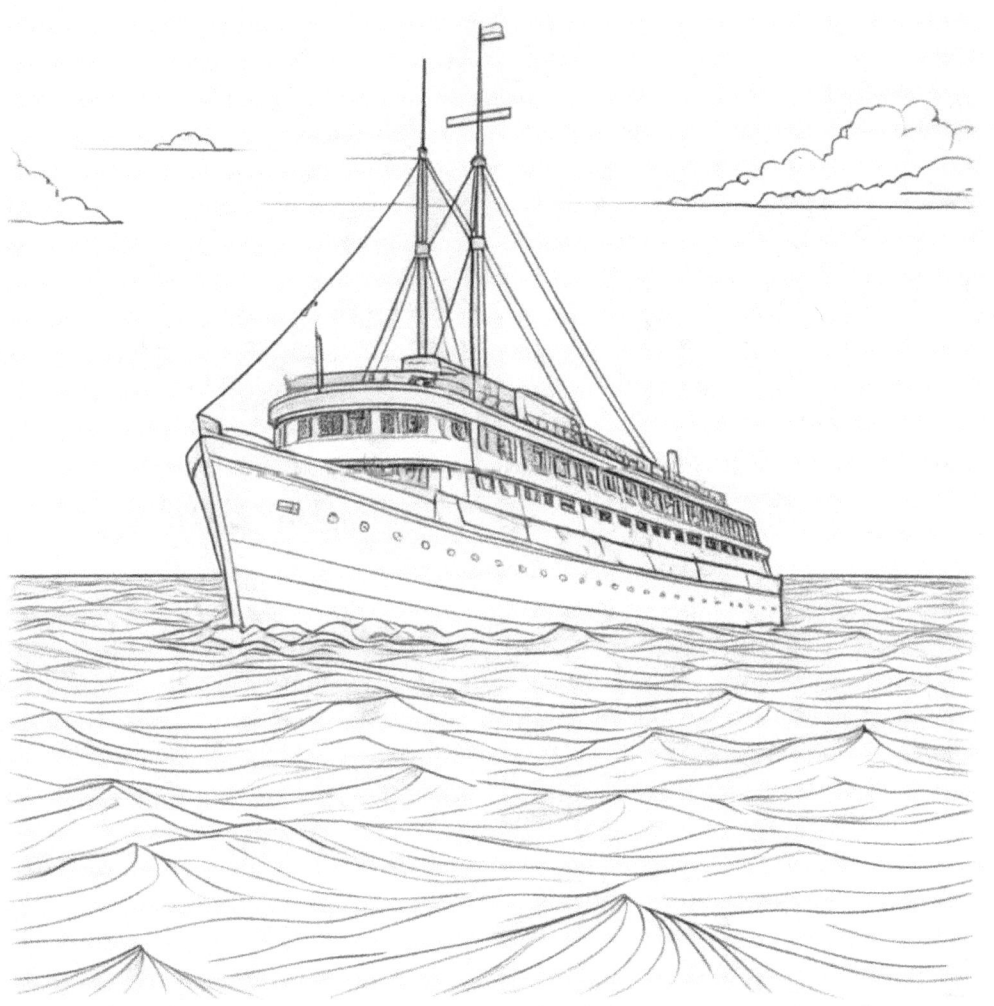

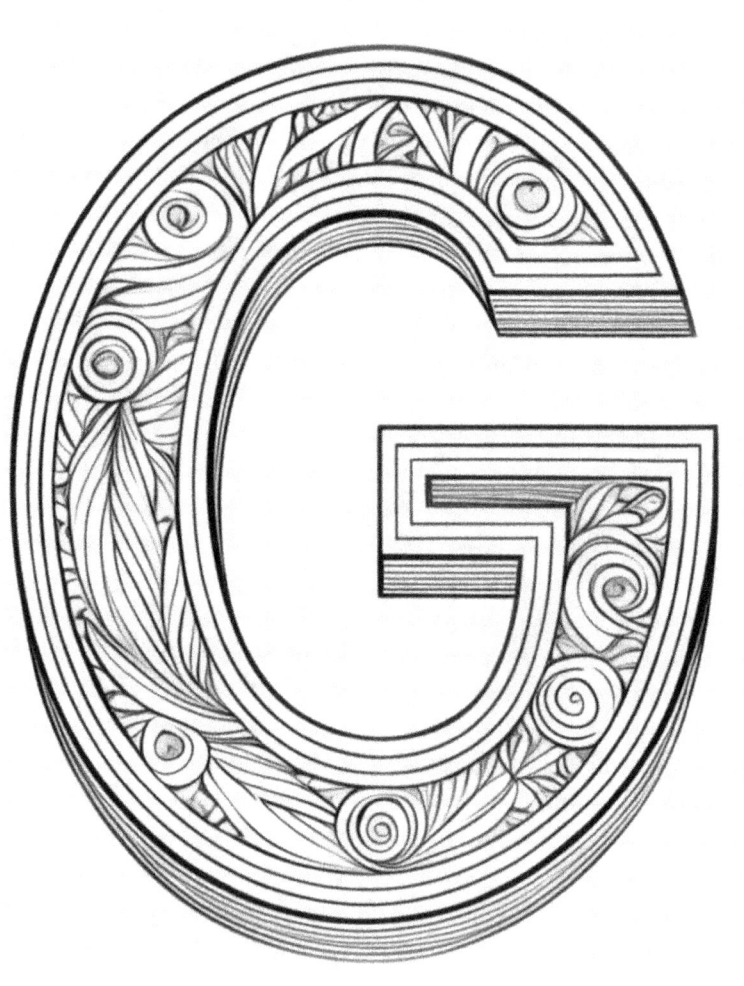

Gorilla

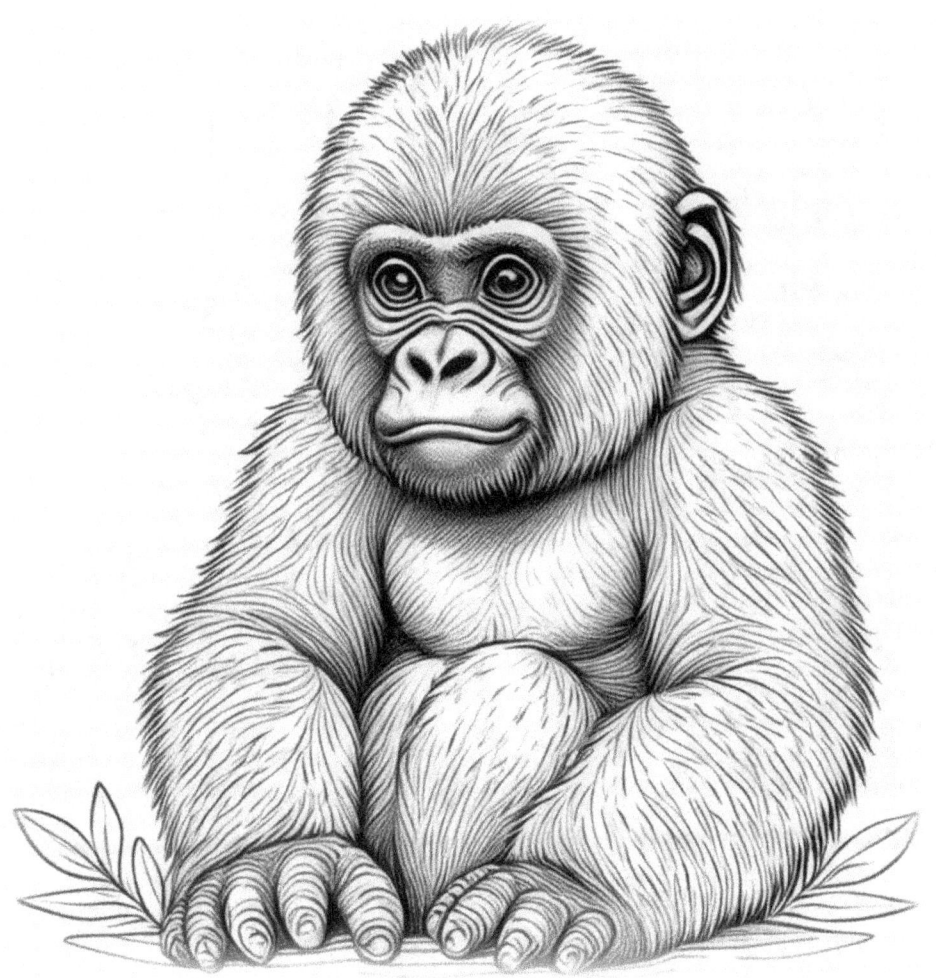

Grape

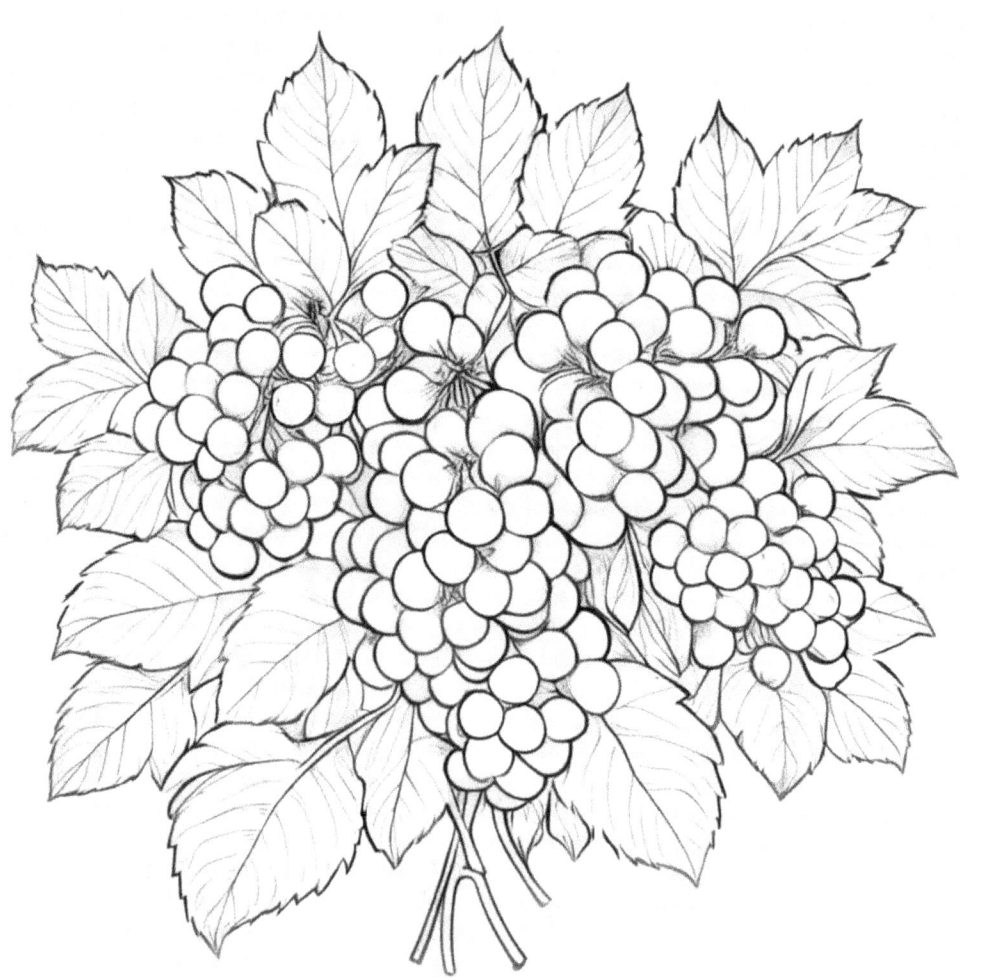

Glider

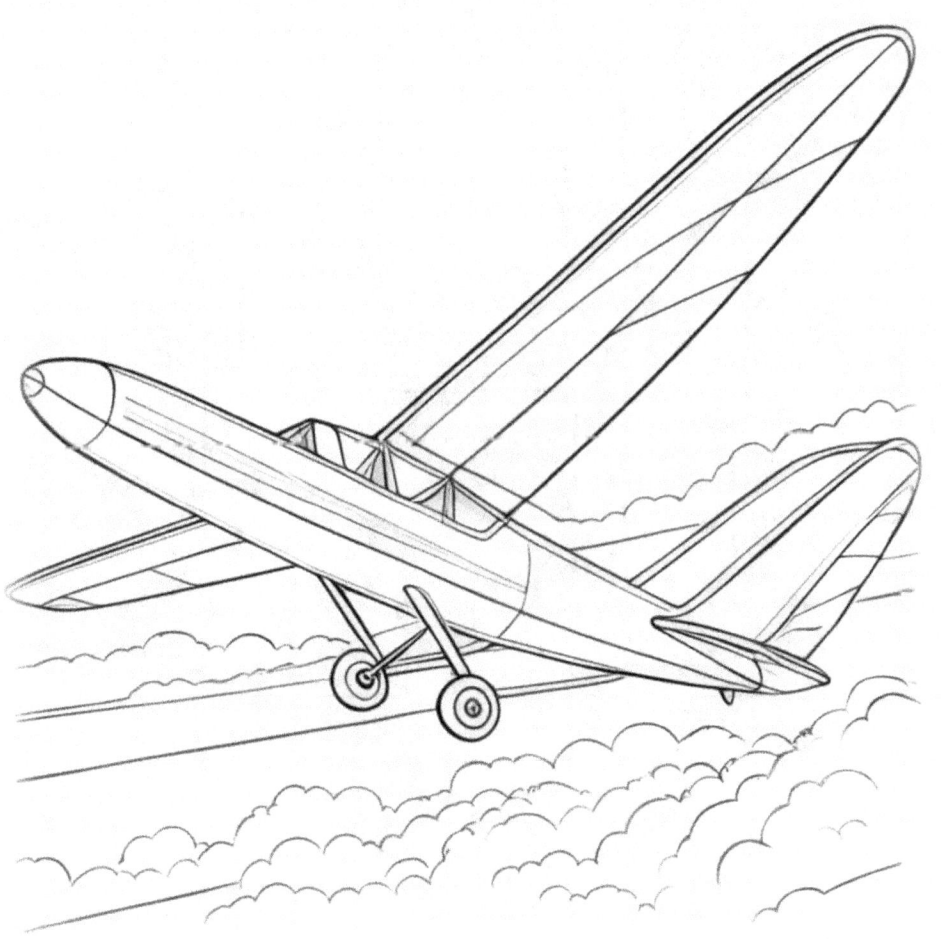

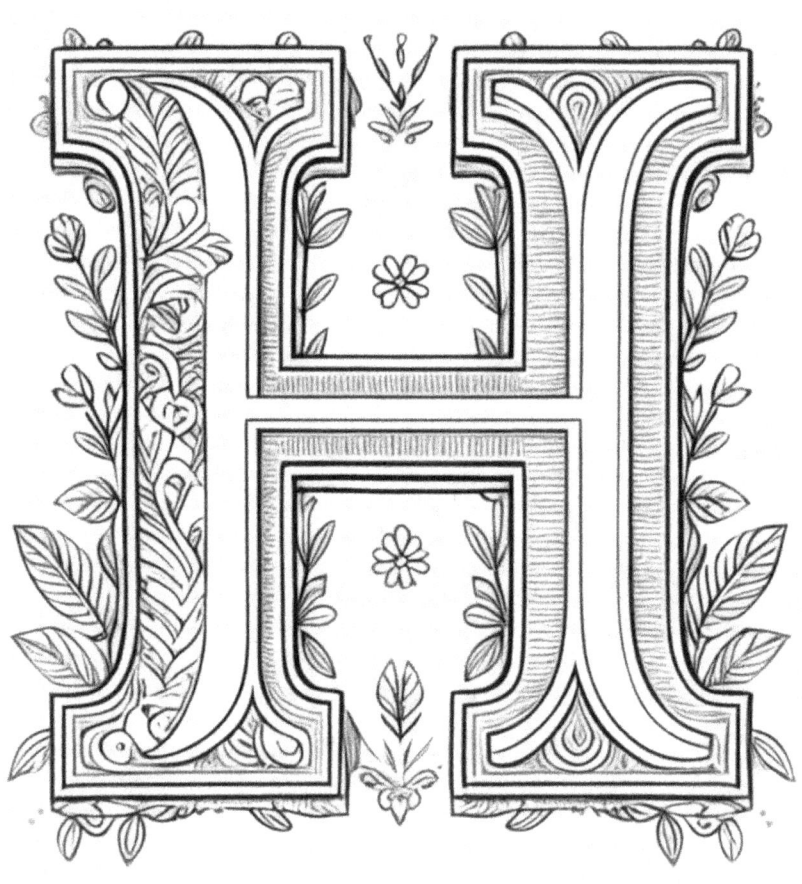

Horse

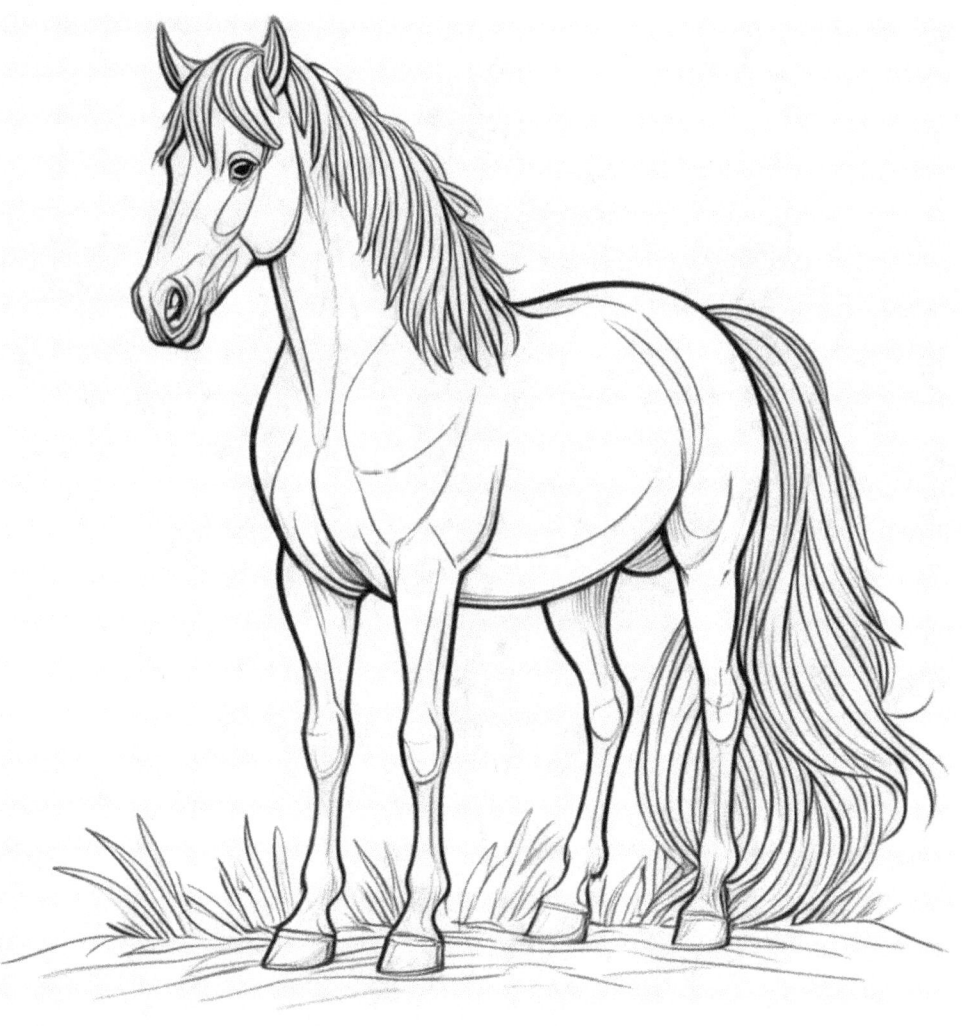

Hyacinth

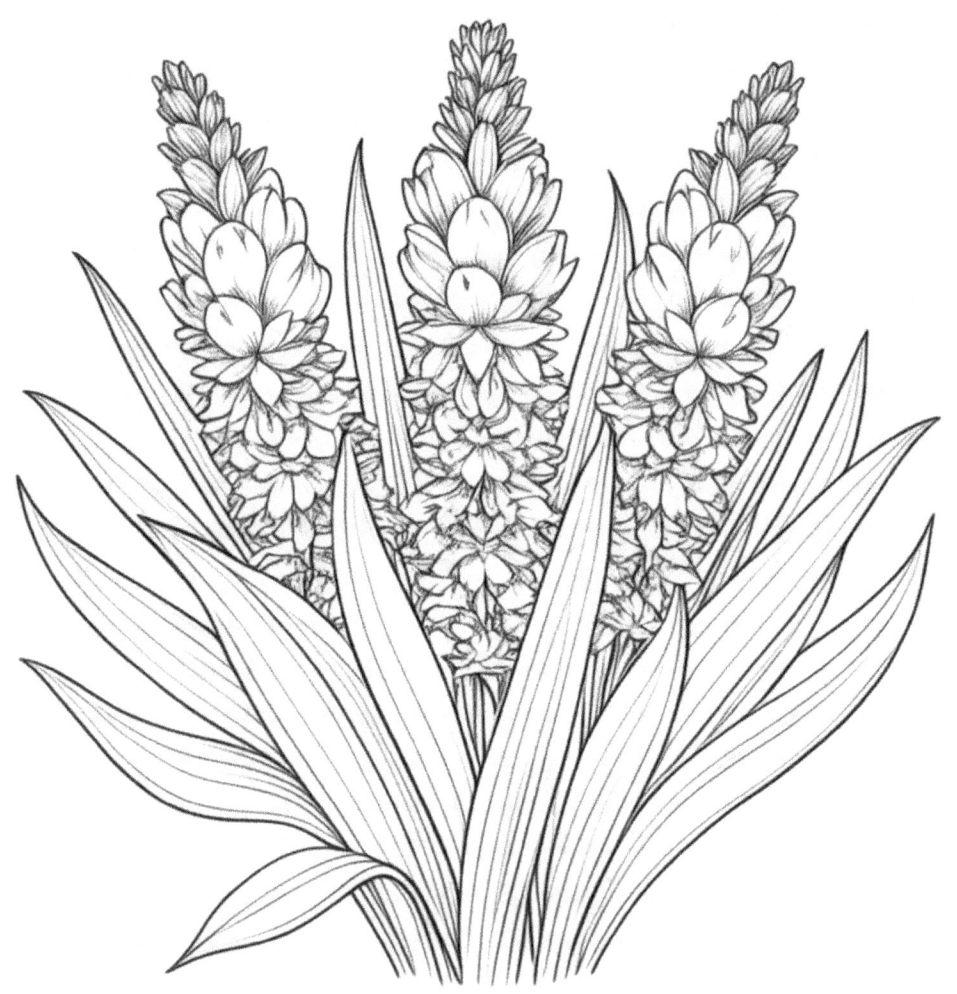

Helicopter

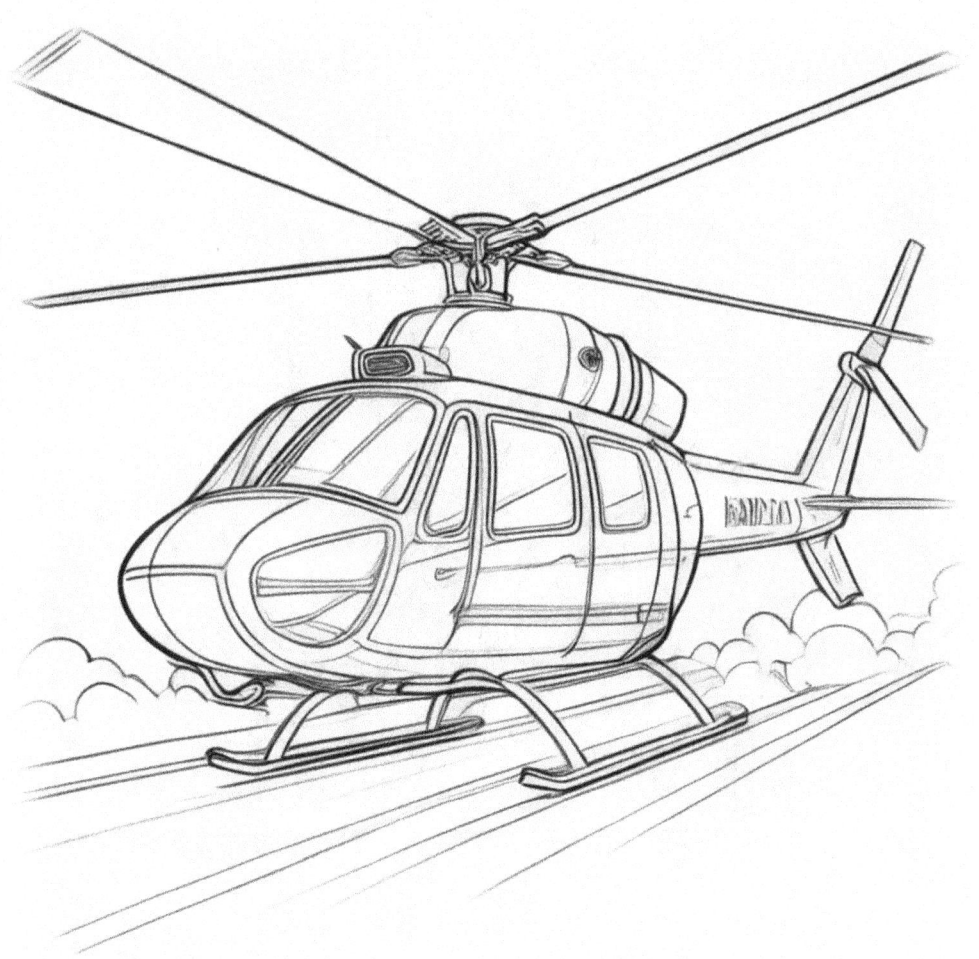

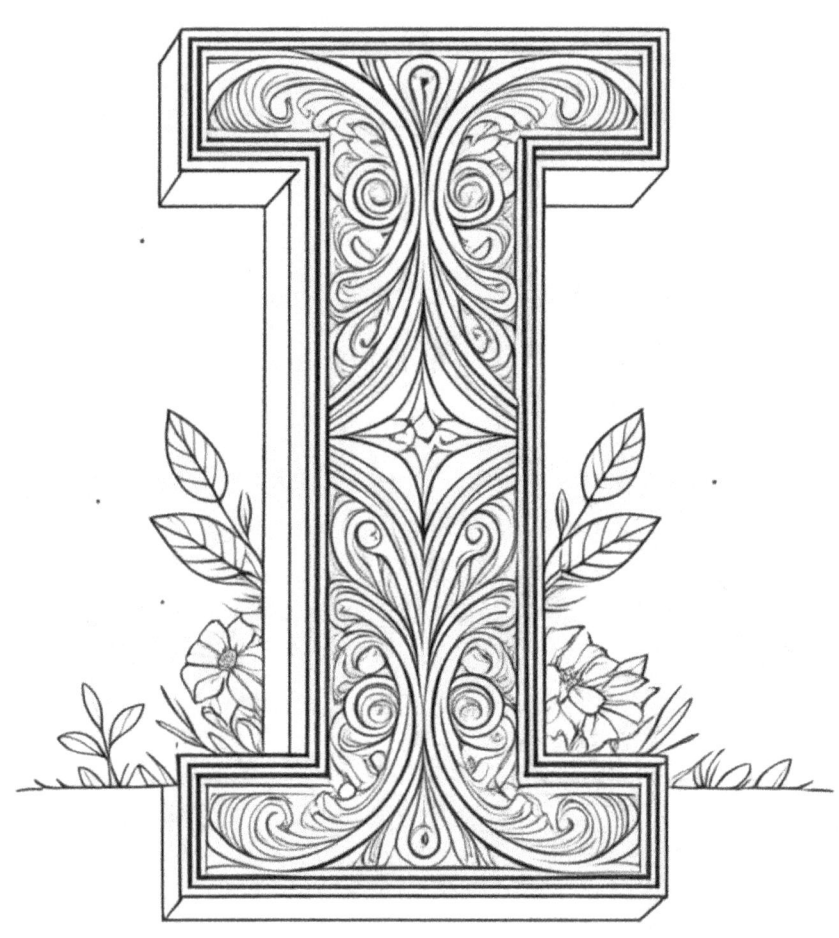

Impala

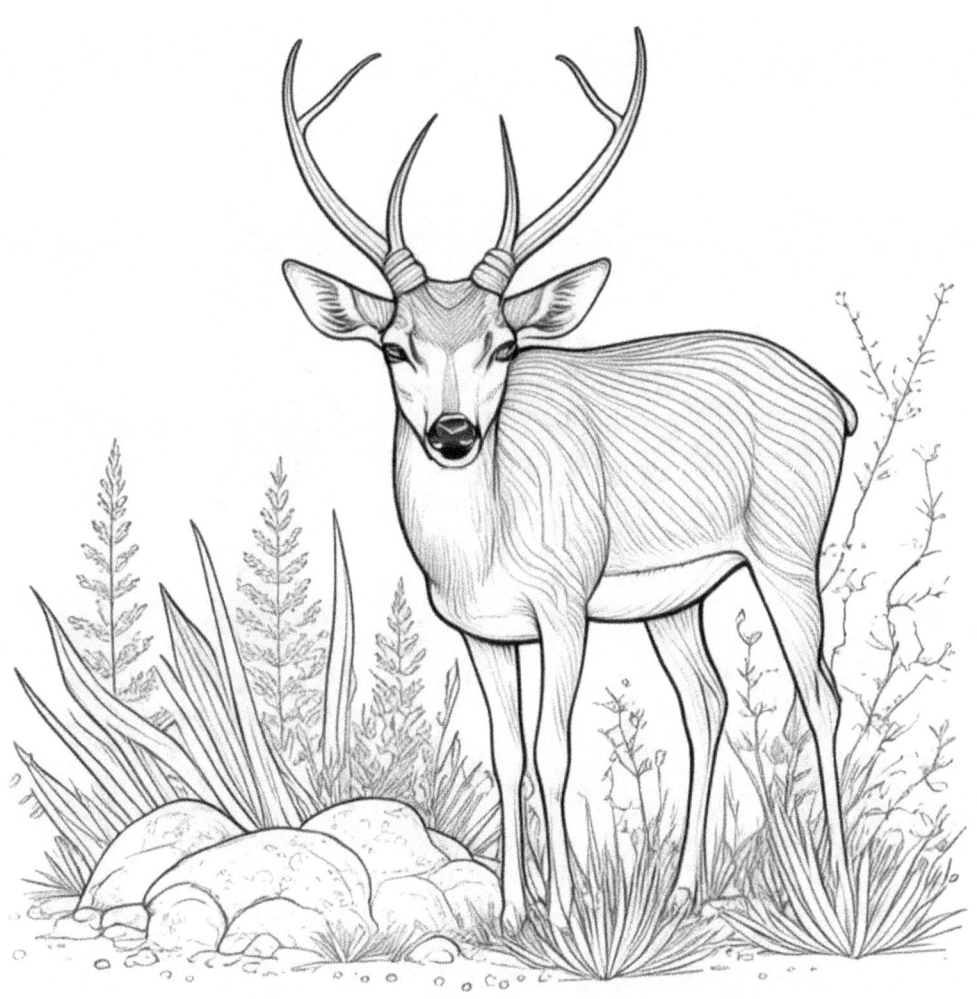

Iris

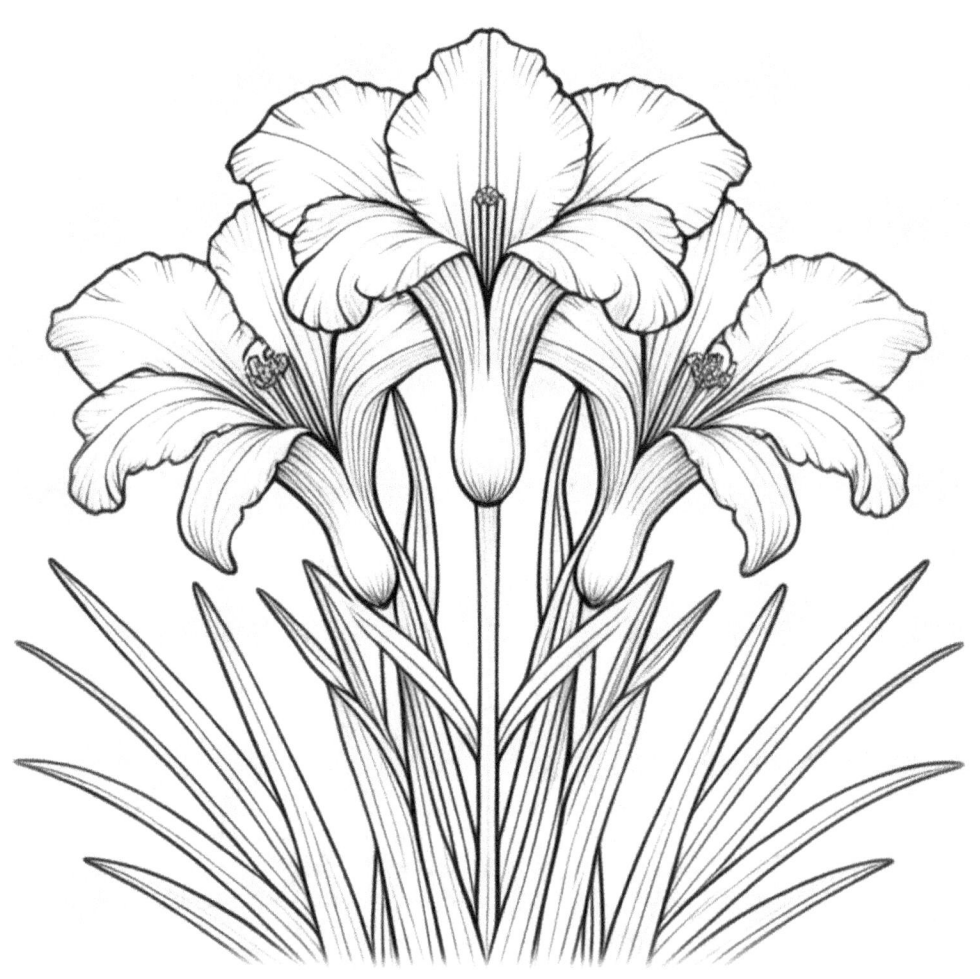

Interceptor

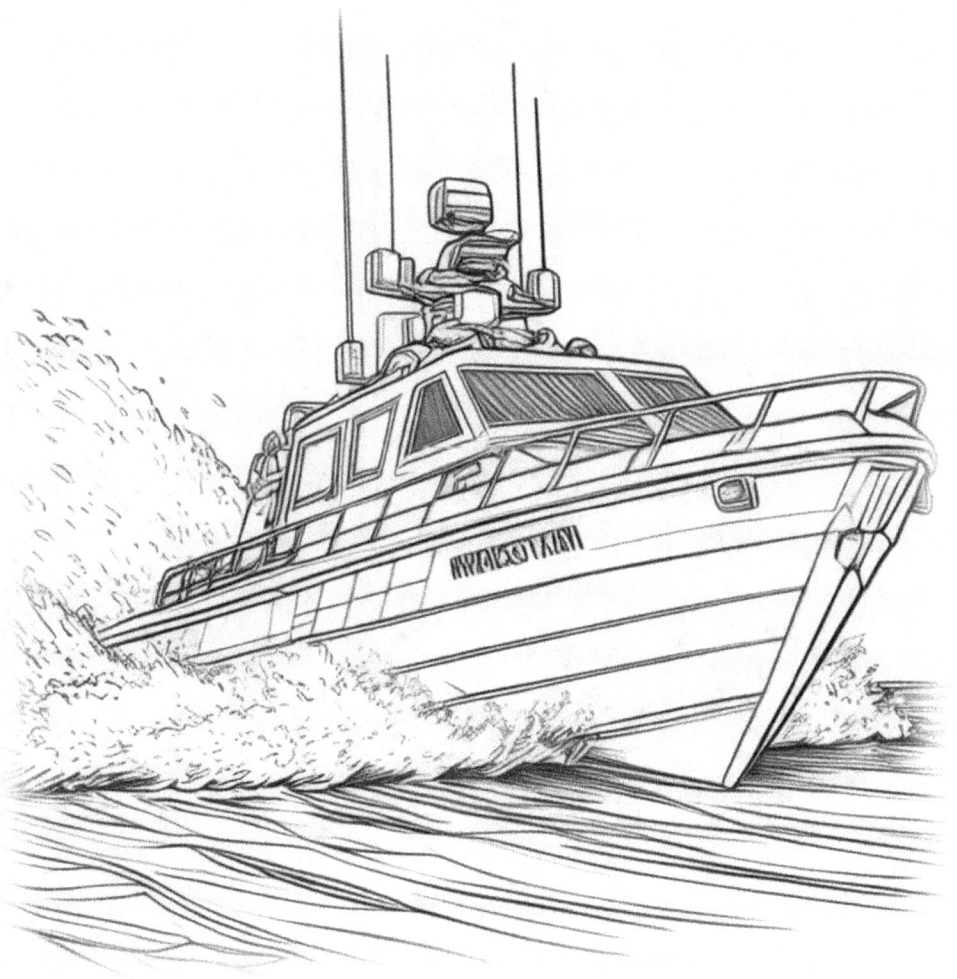

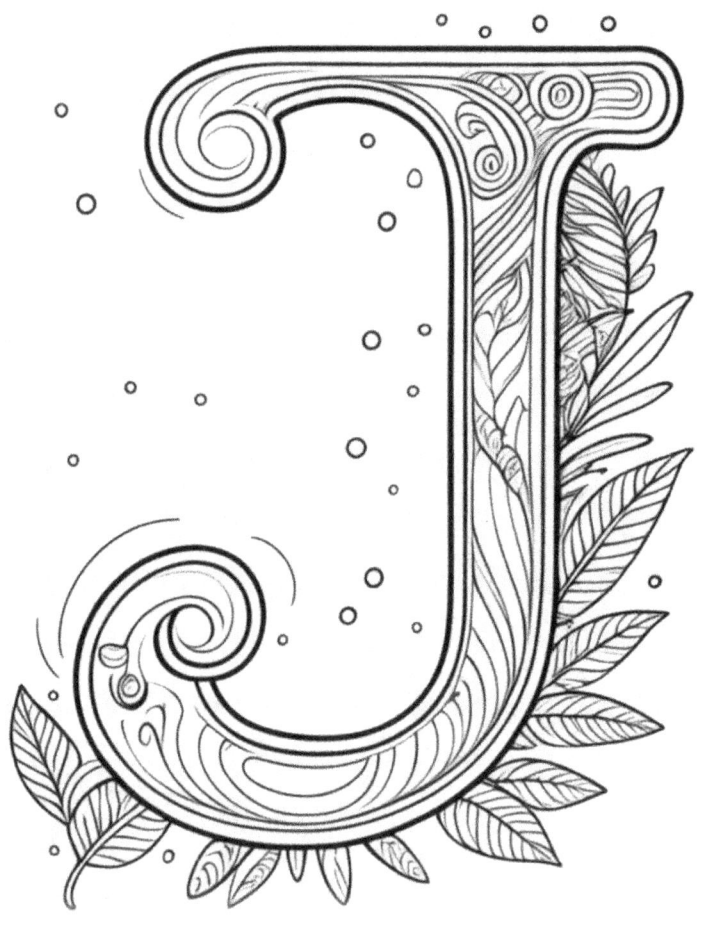

Jaguar

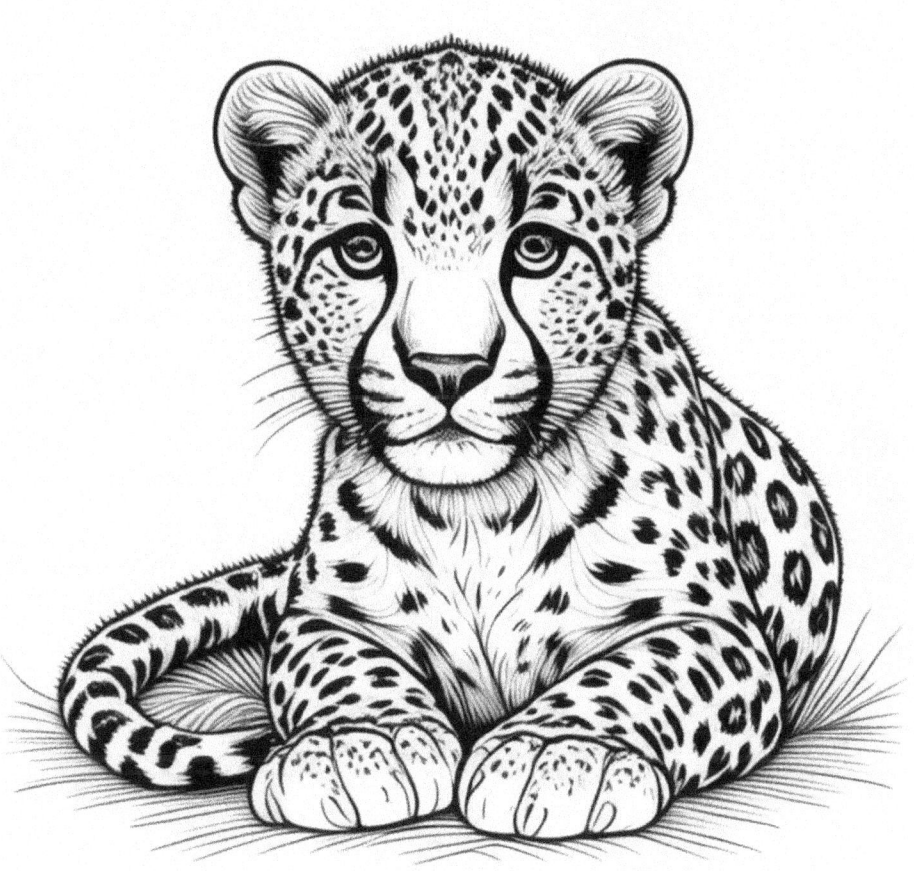

Jasmine

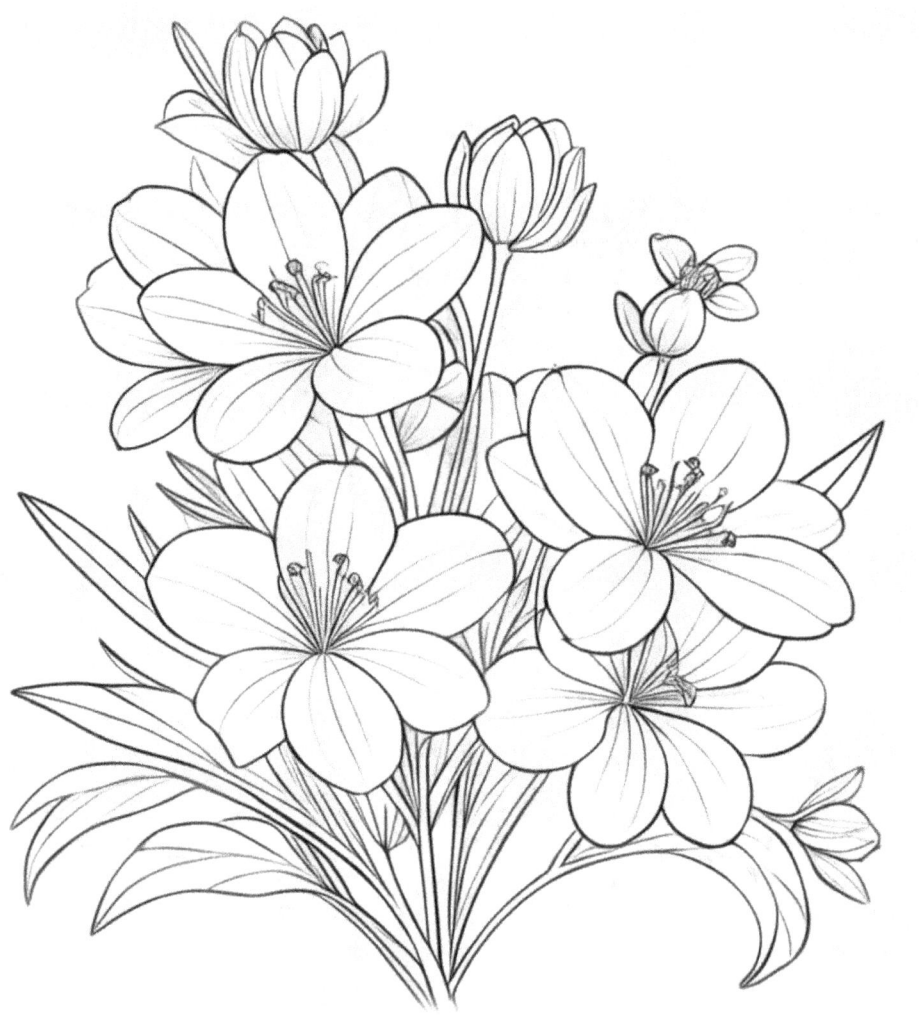

Jet

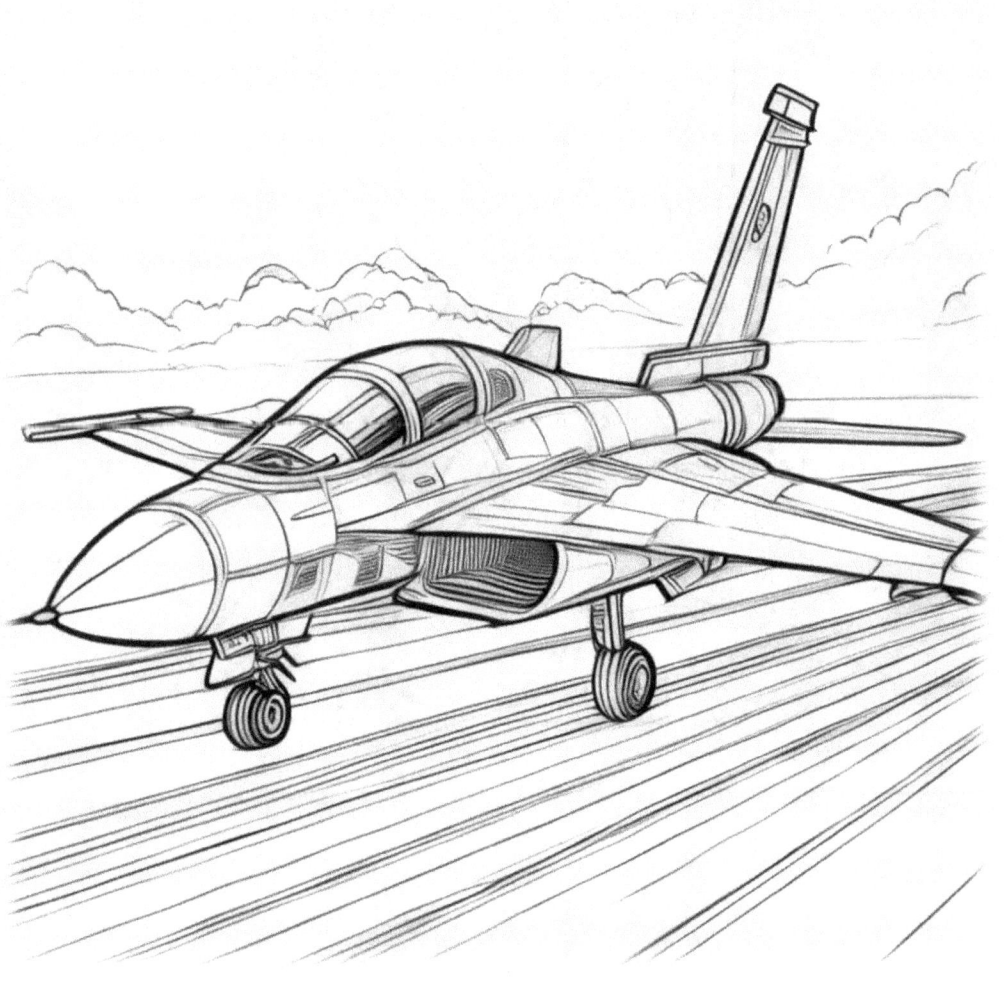

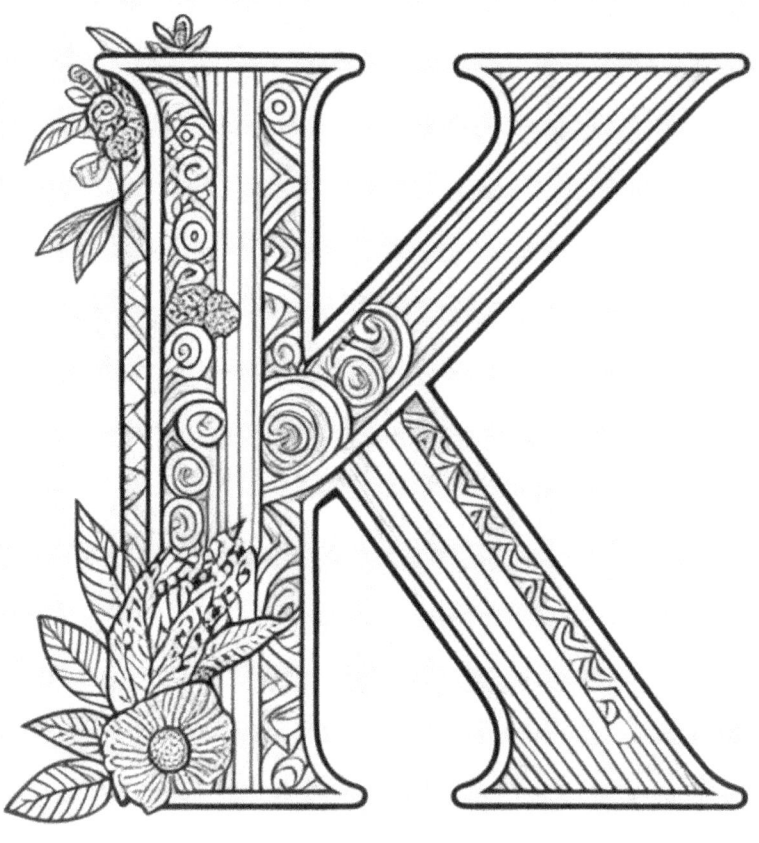

Koala

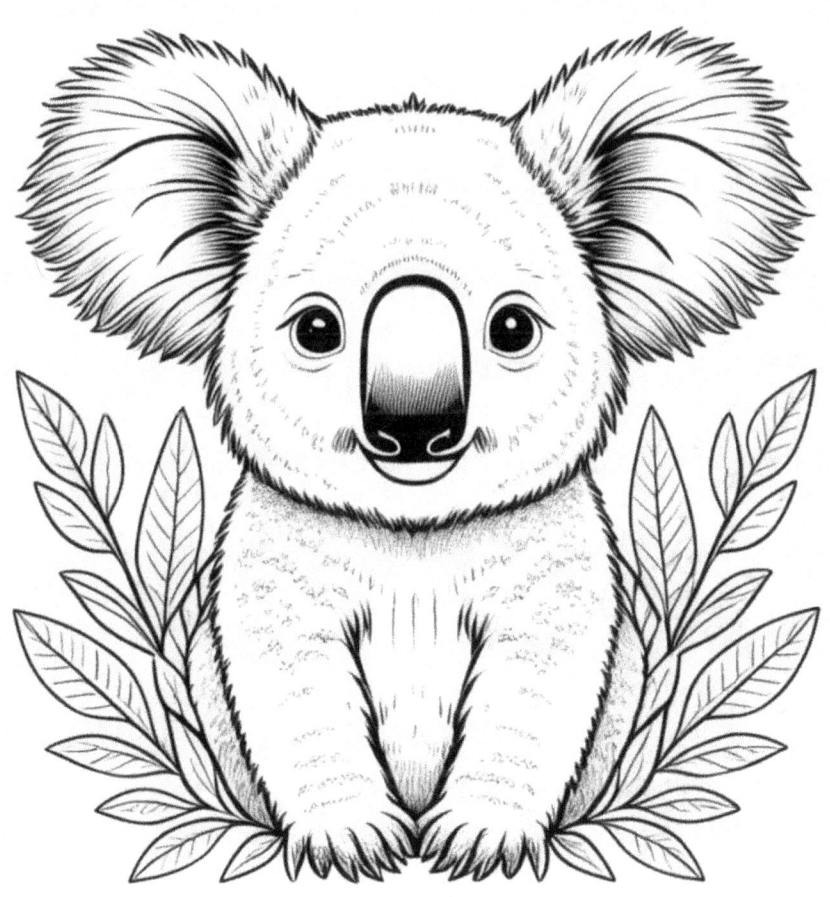

Kiwi

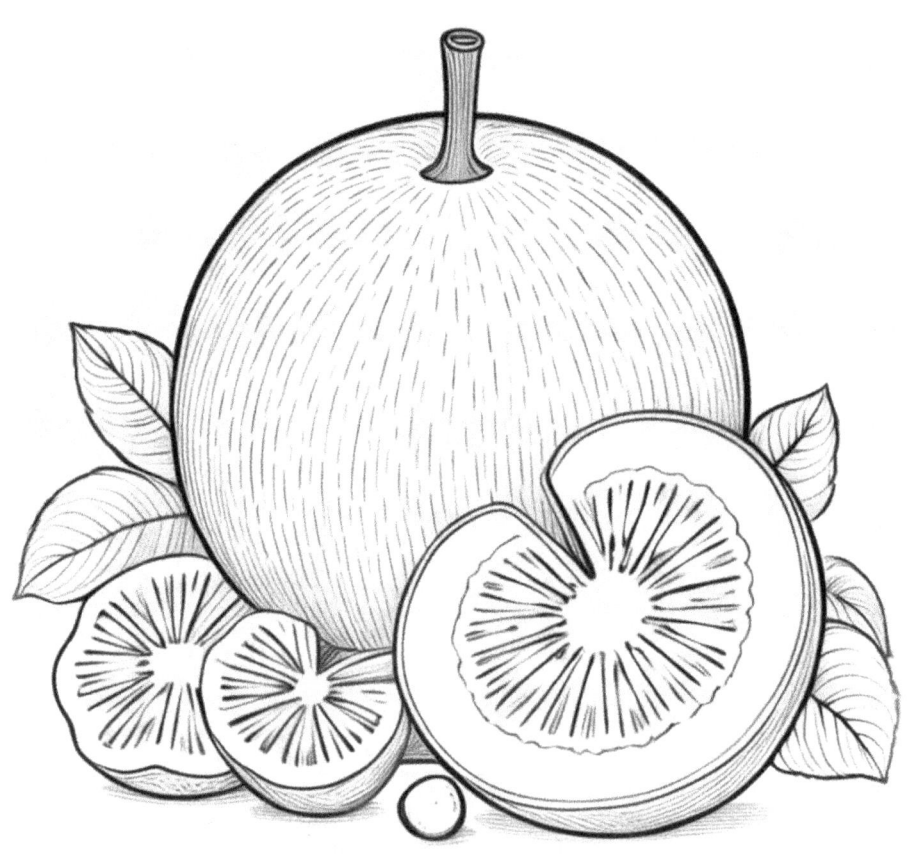

Kayak

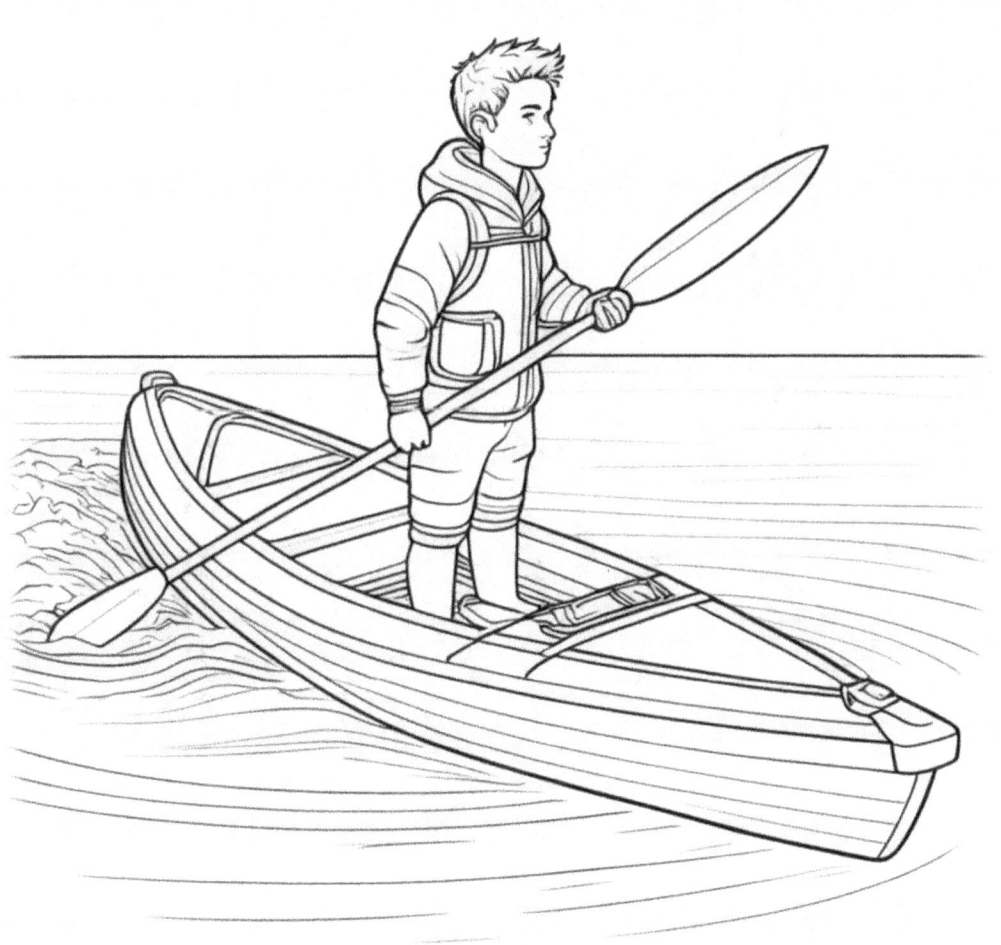

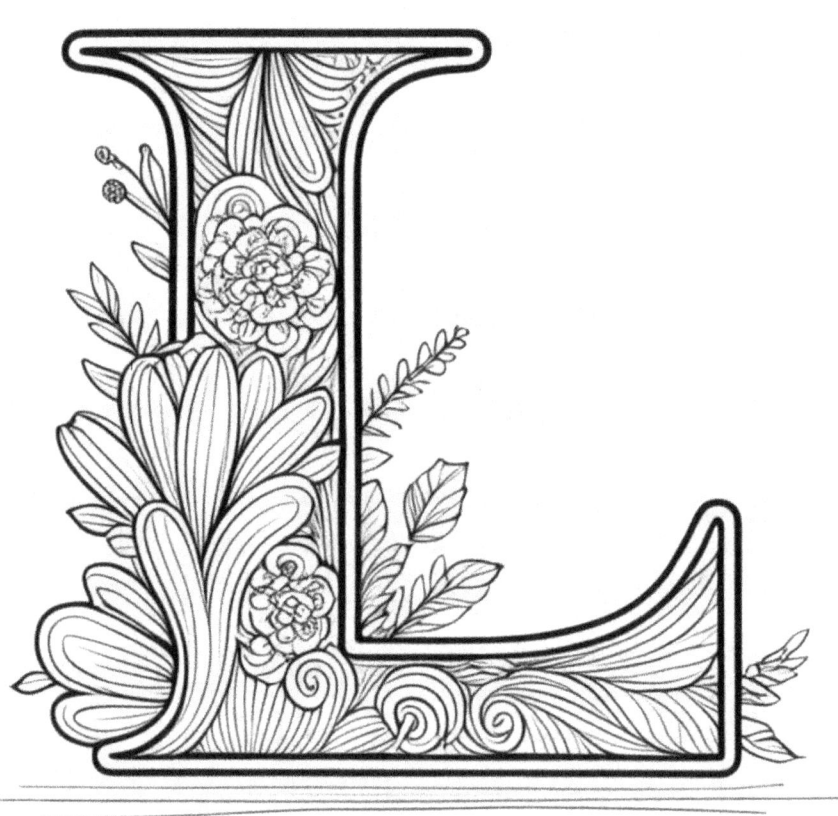

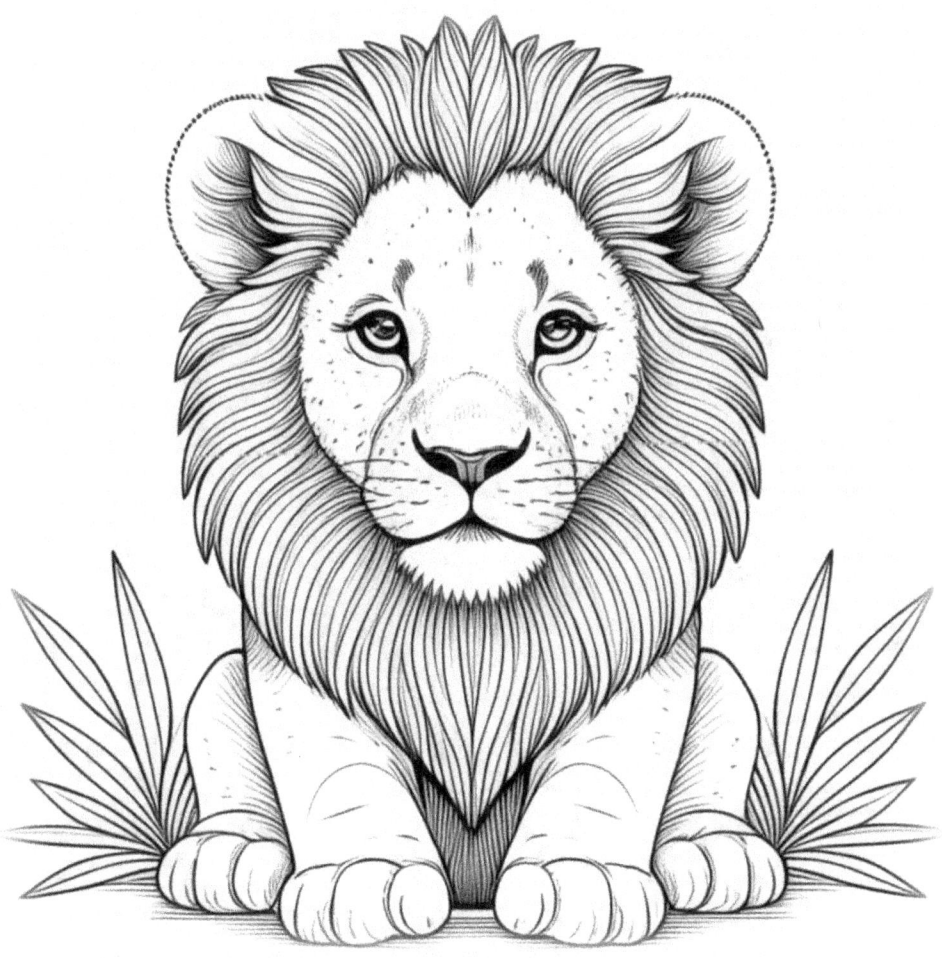

Lemon

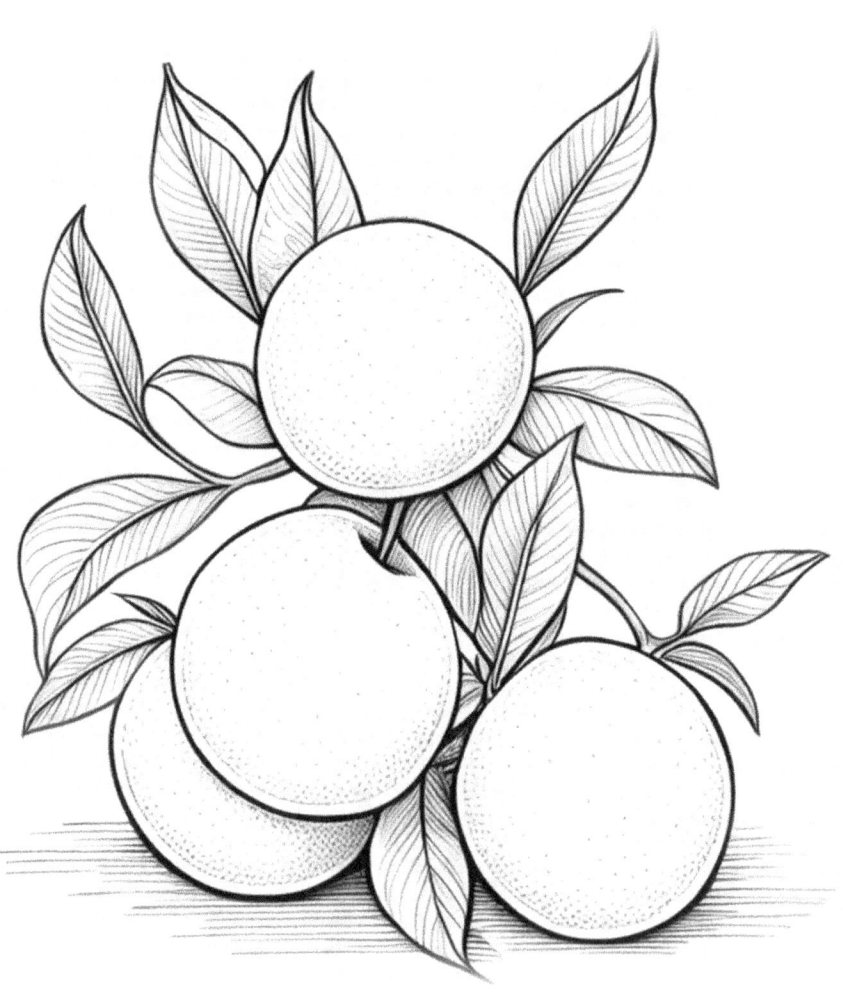

Lorry

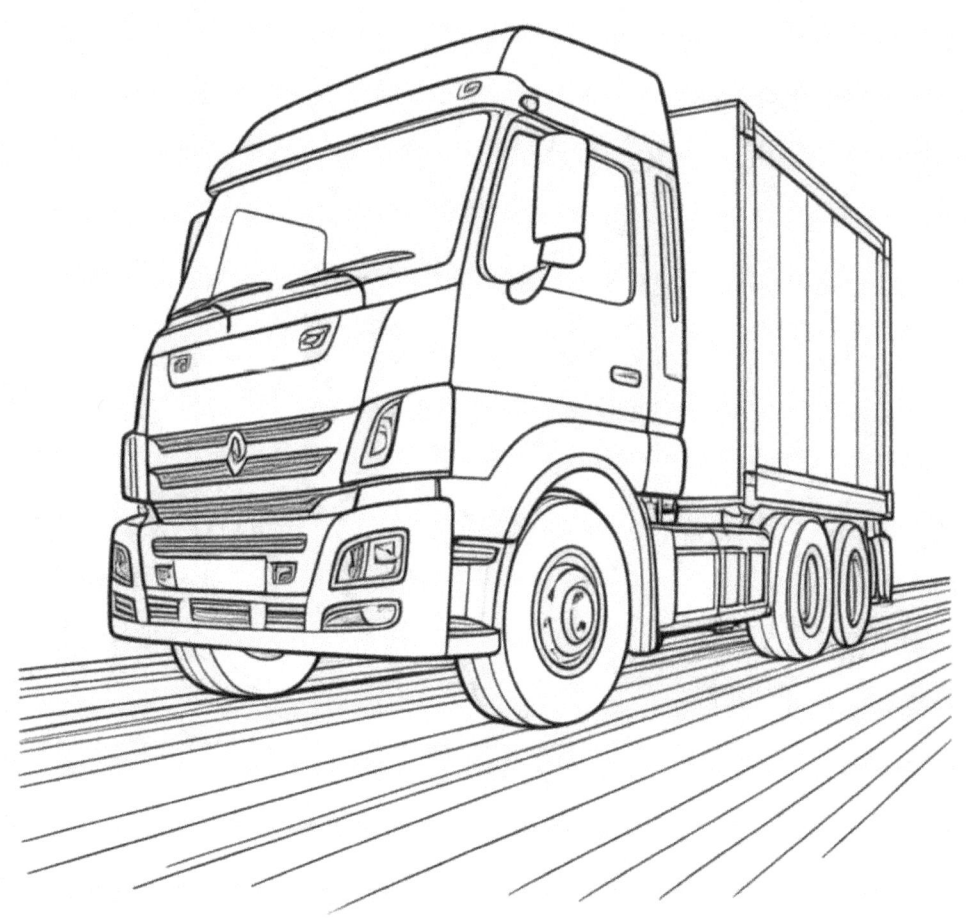

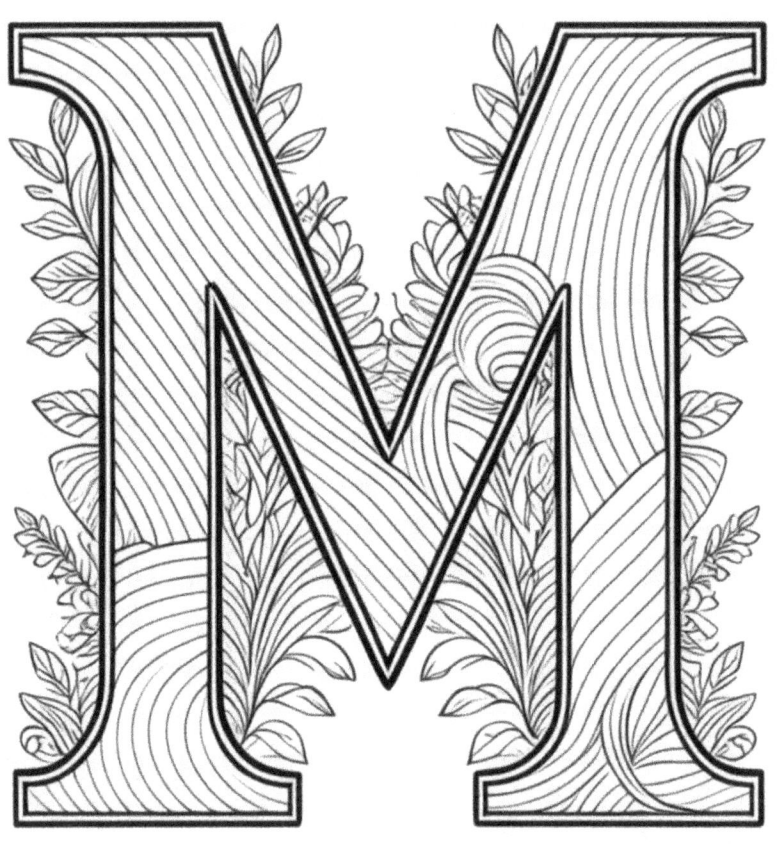

Monkey

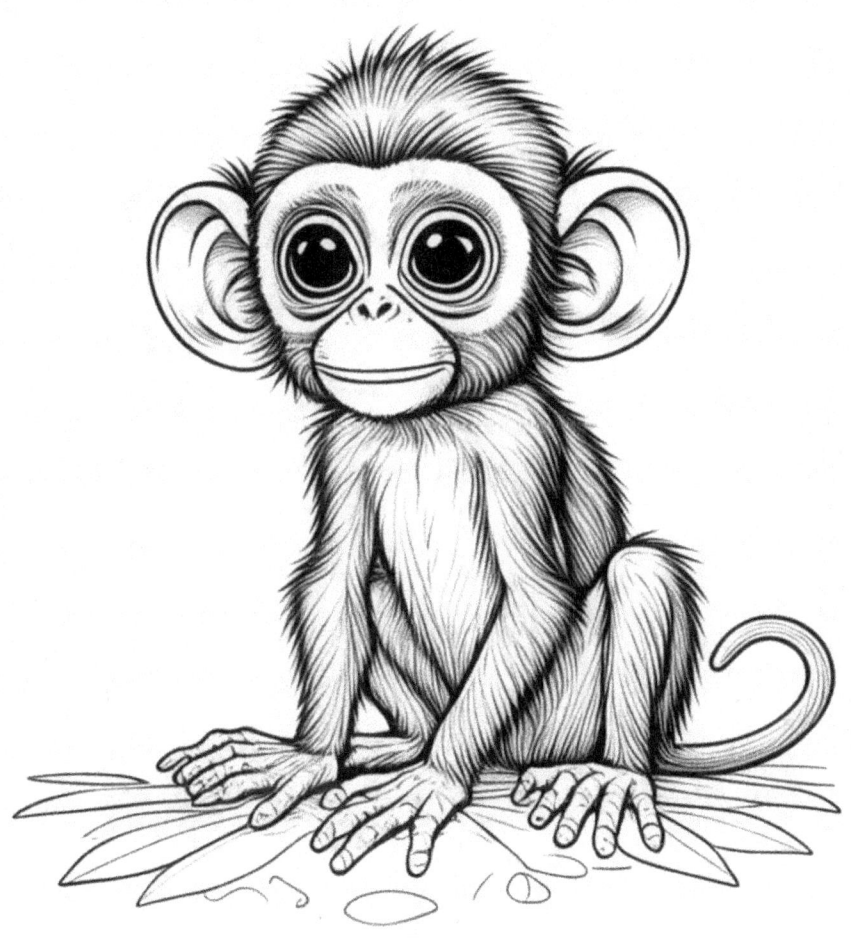

Mango

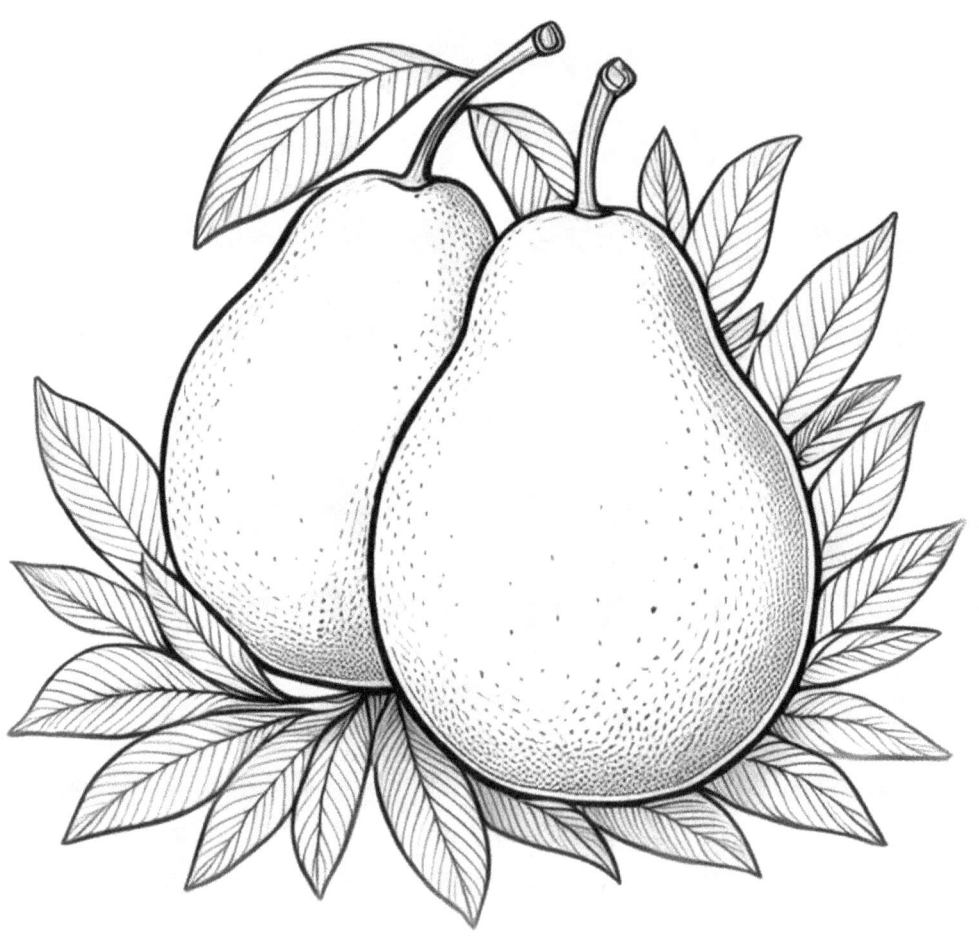

Motorcycle

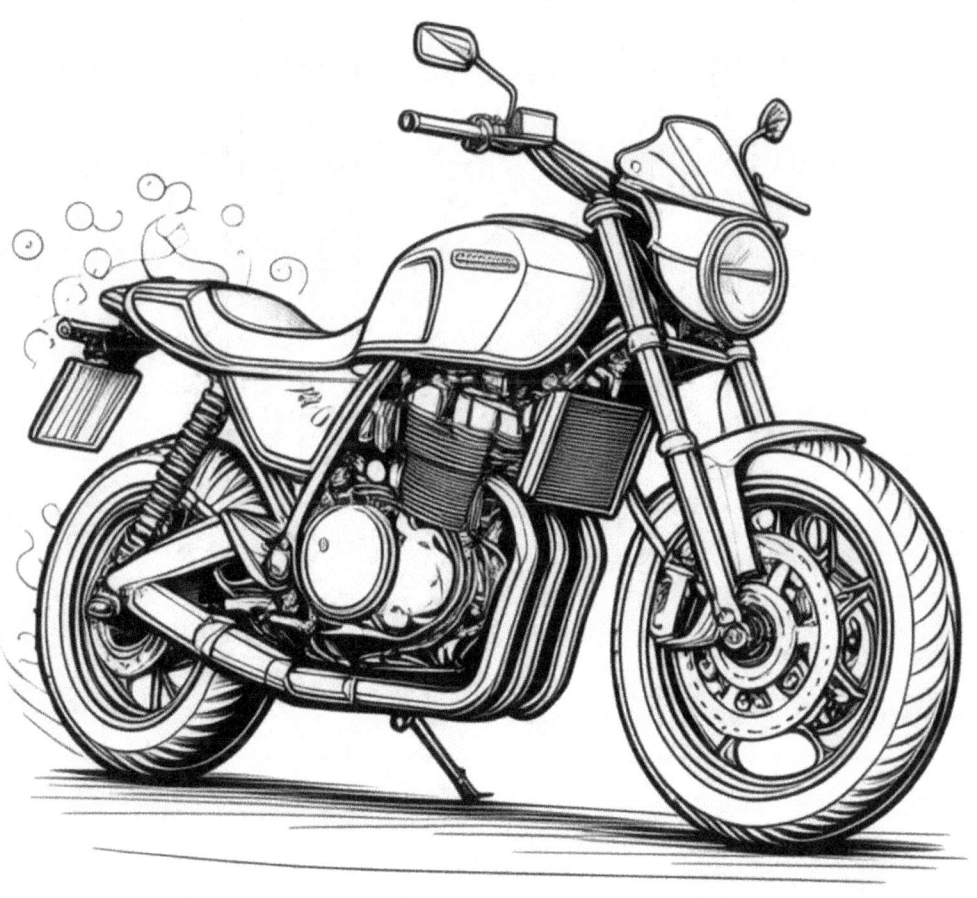

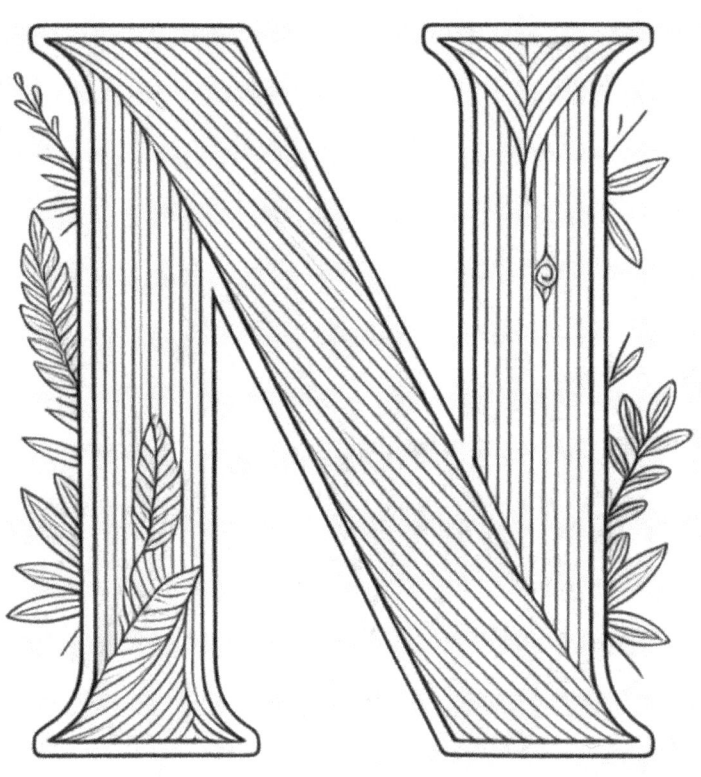

Nutria

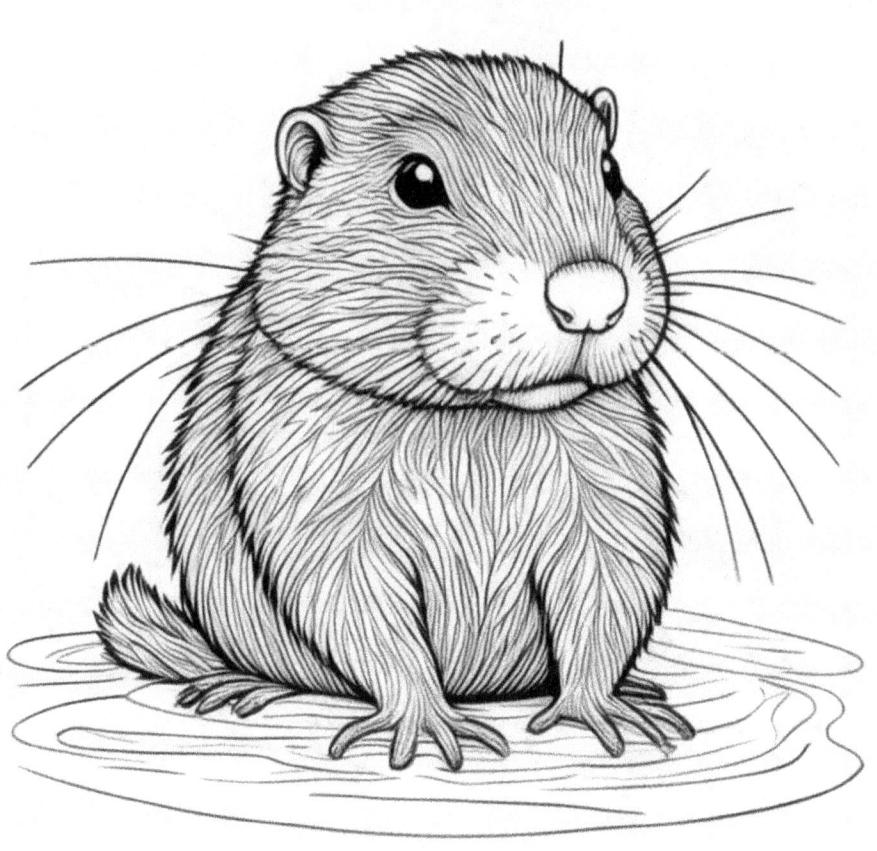

Nectarine

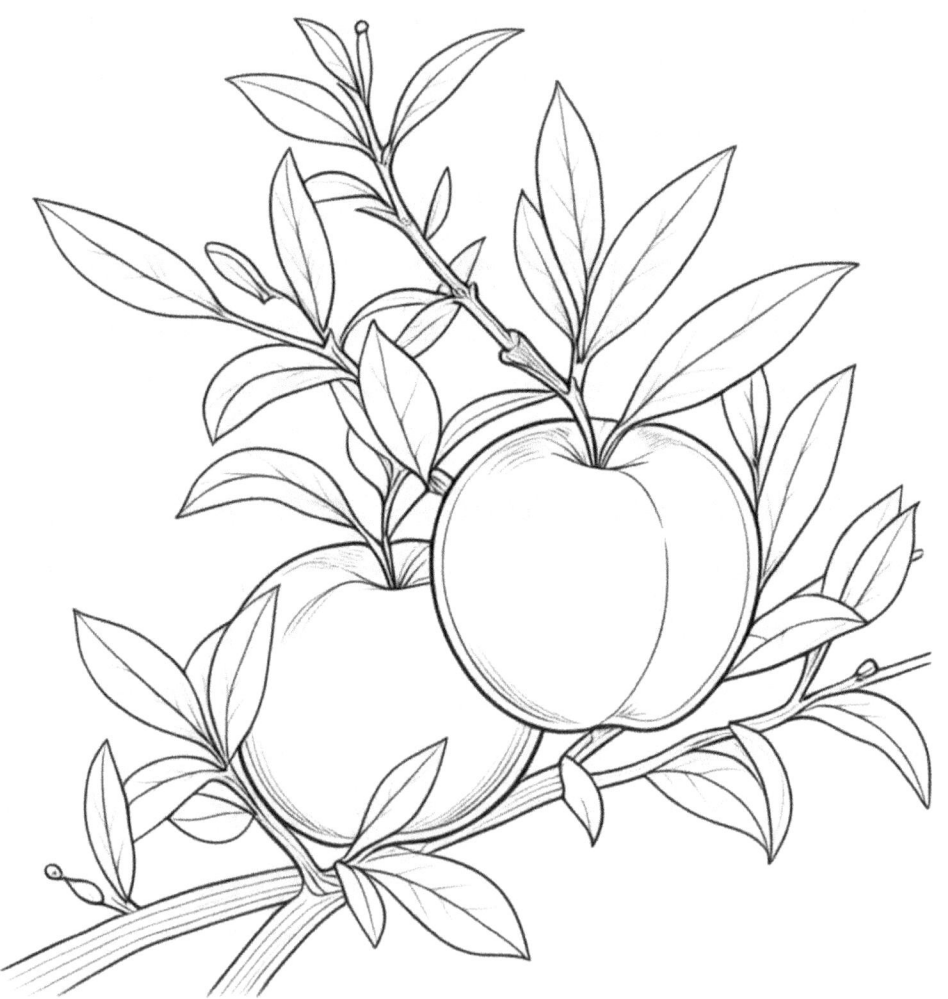

Narrowboat

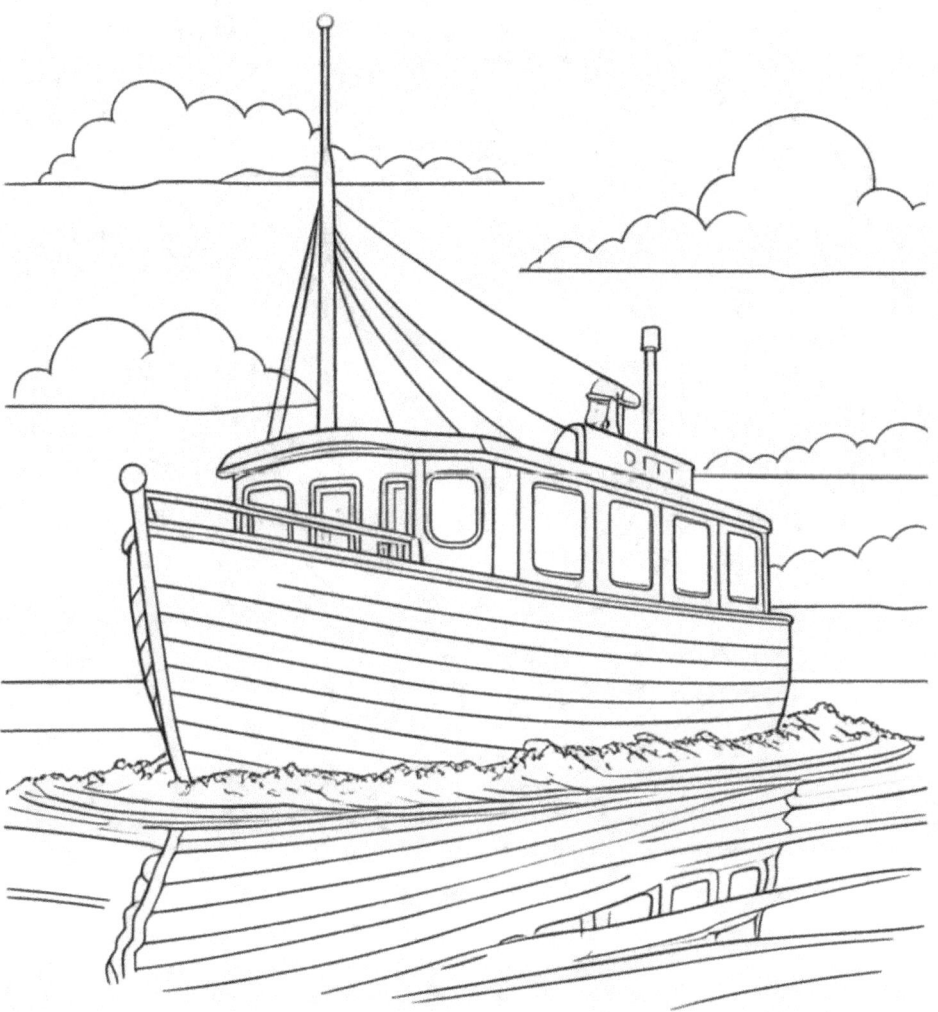

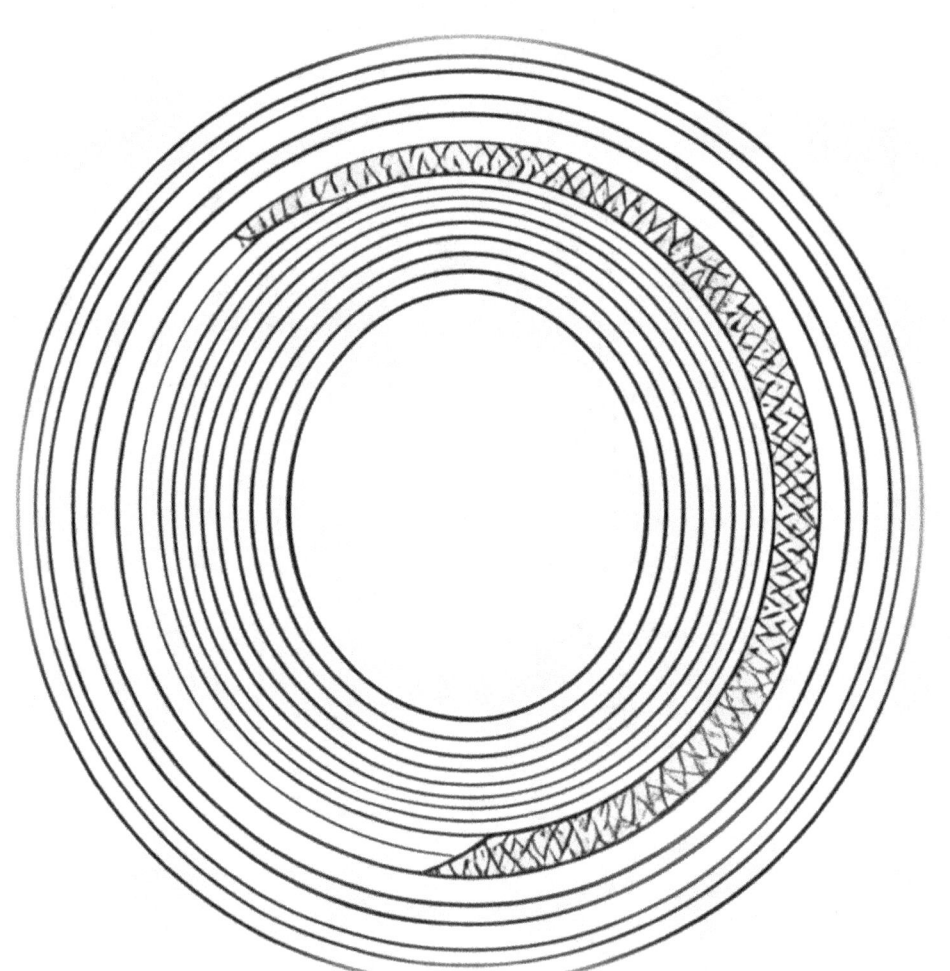

Octopus

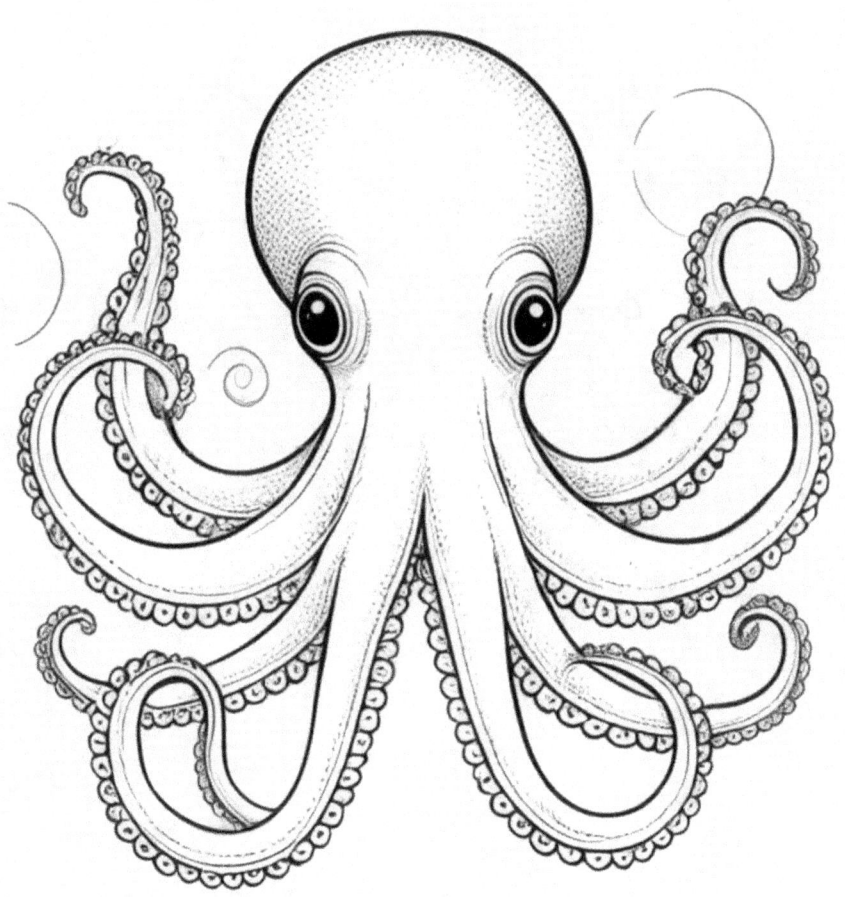

Orange

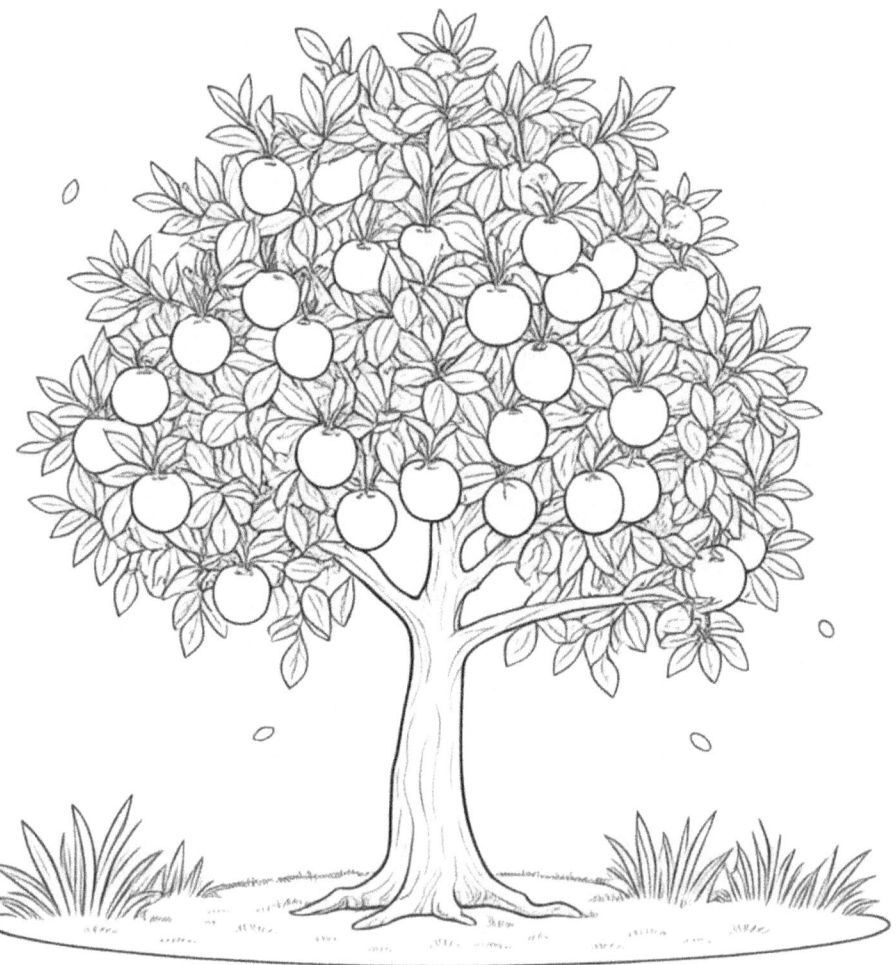

Omnibus

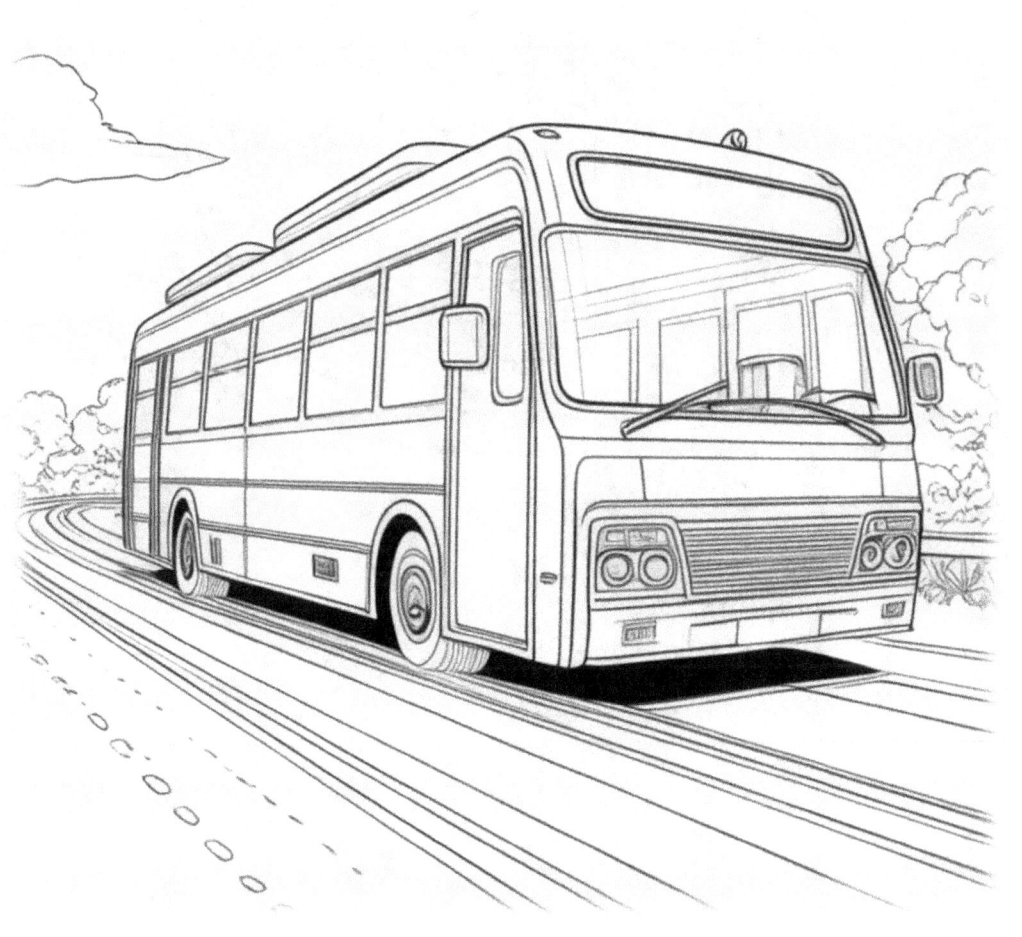

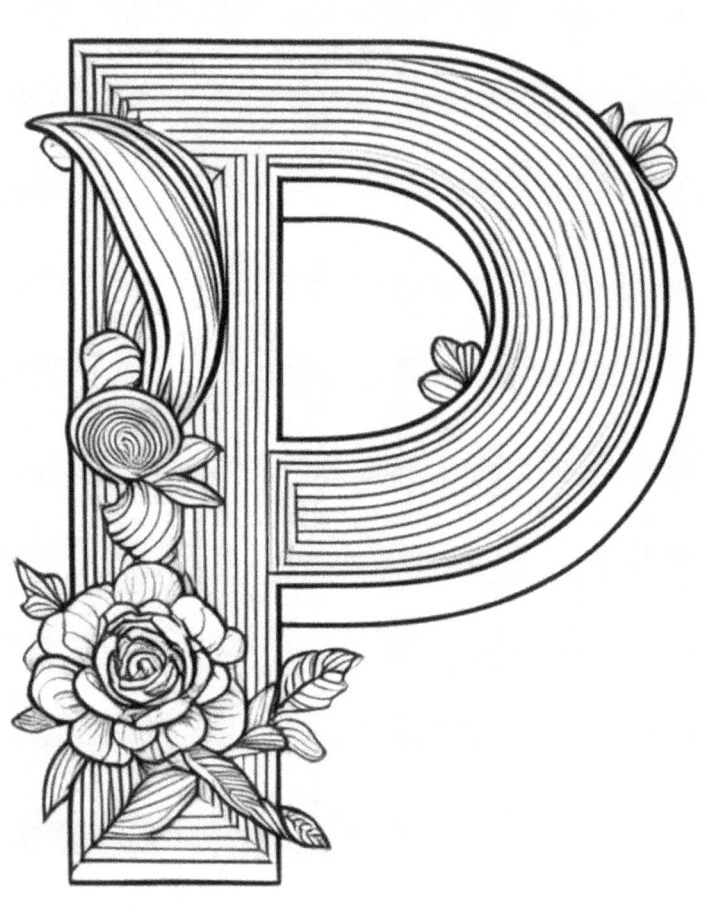

Pelican

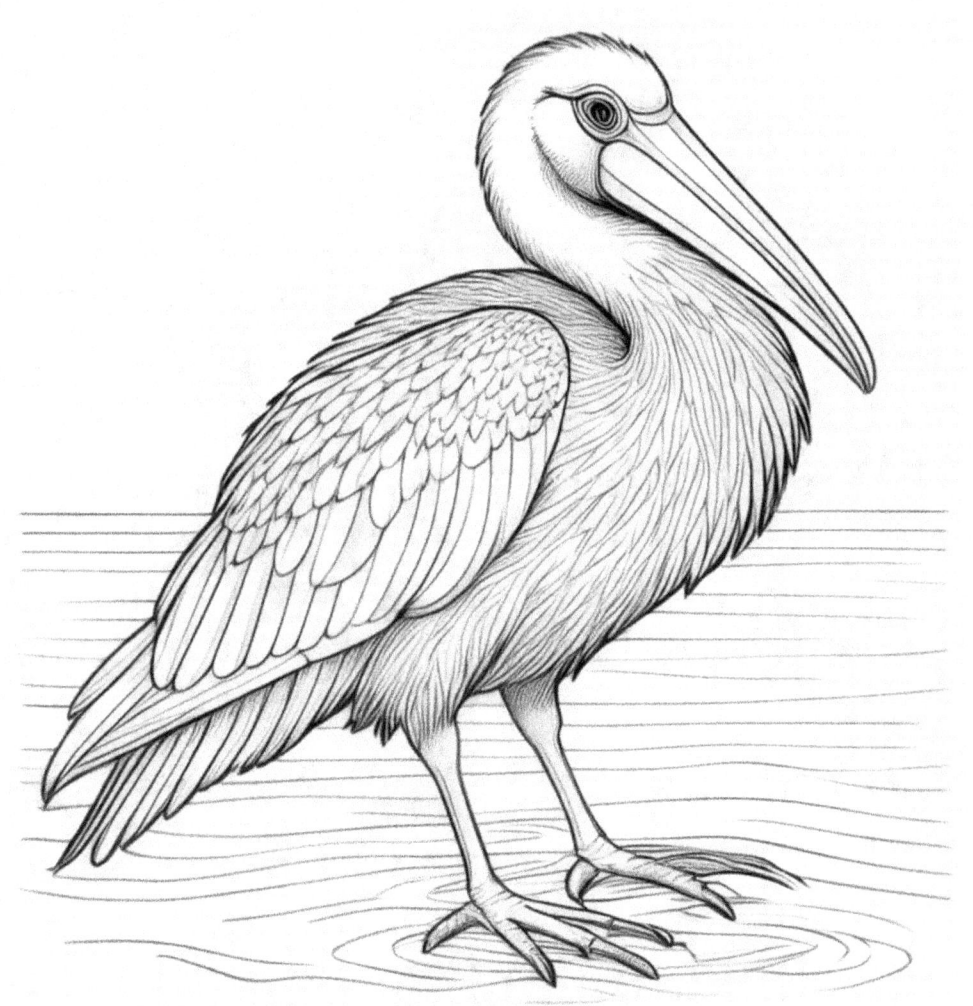

Peach

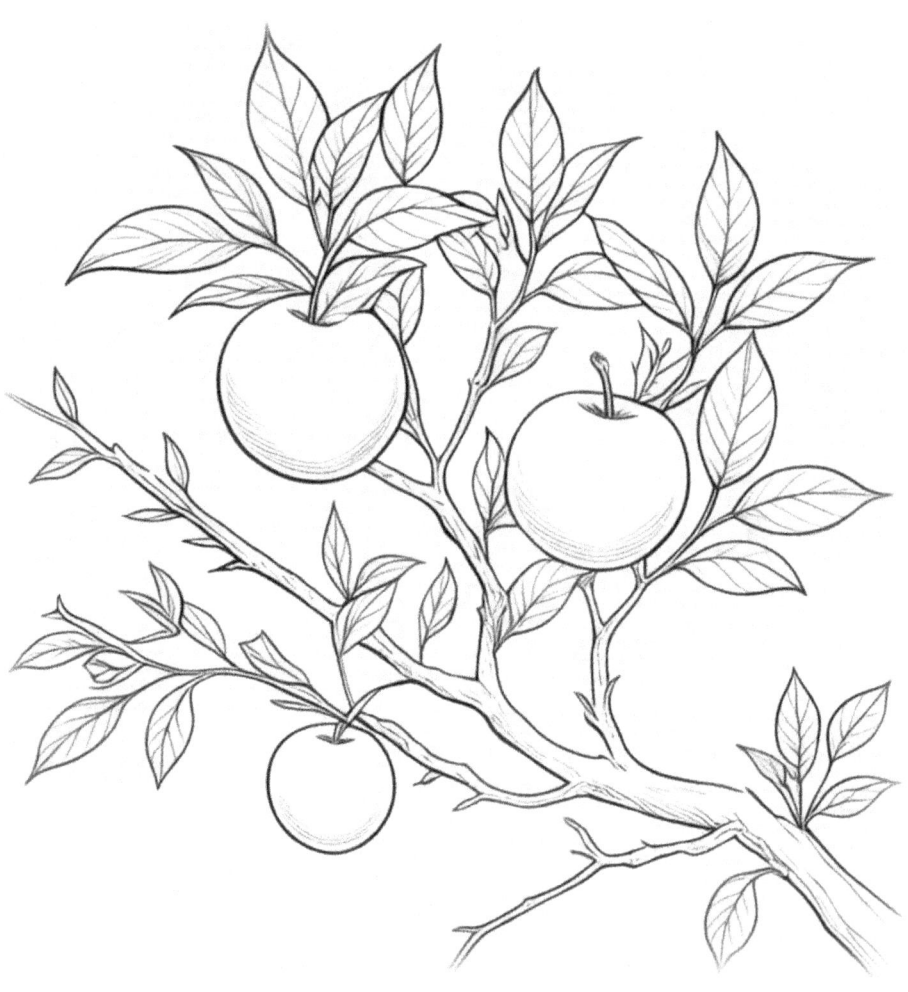

Police car

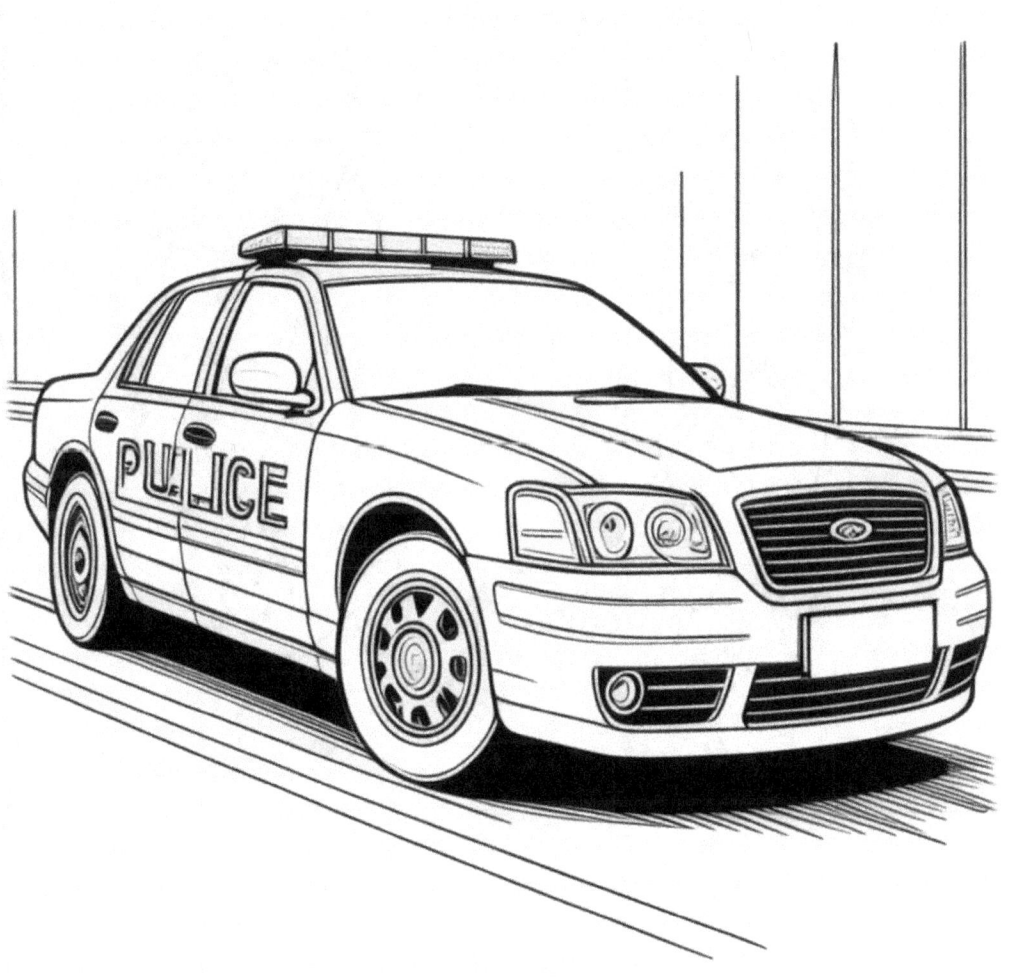

Quail

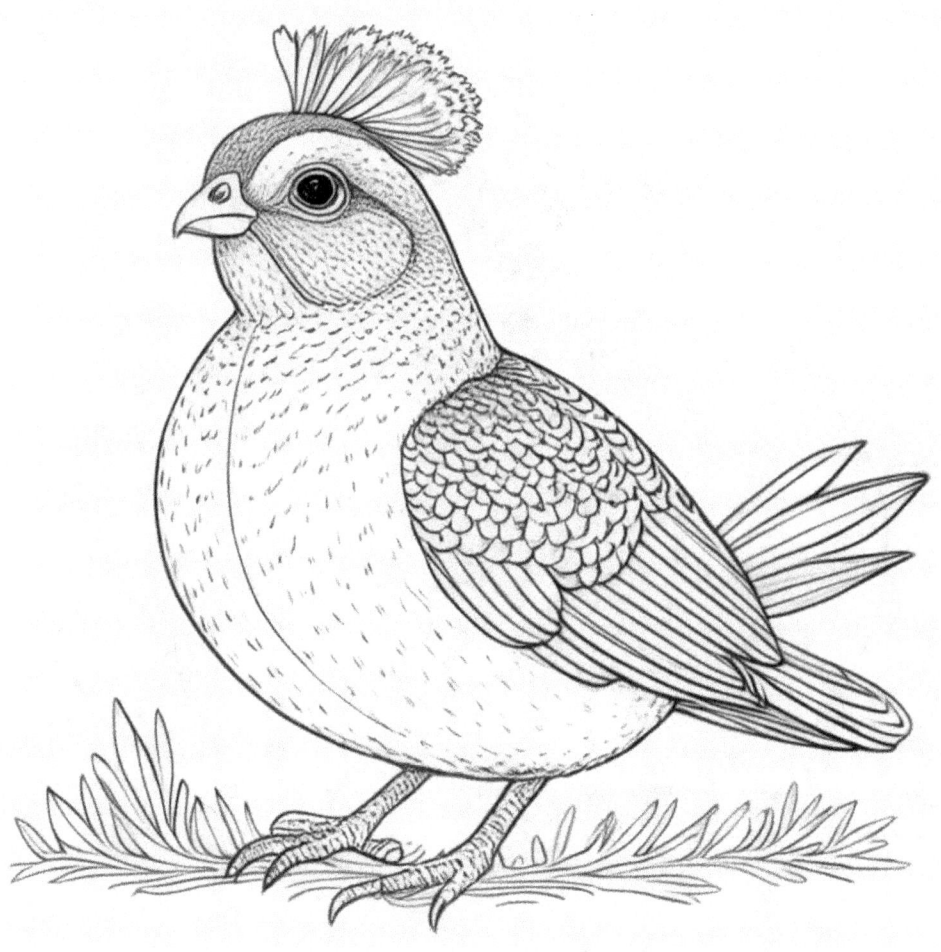

Quince

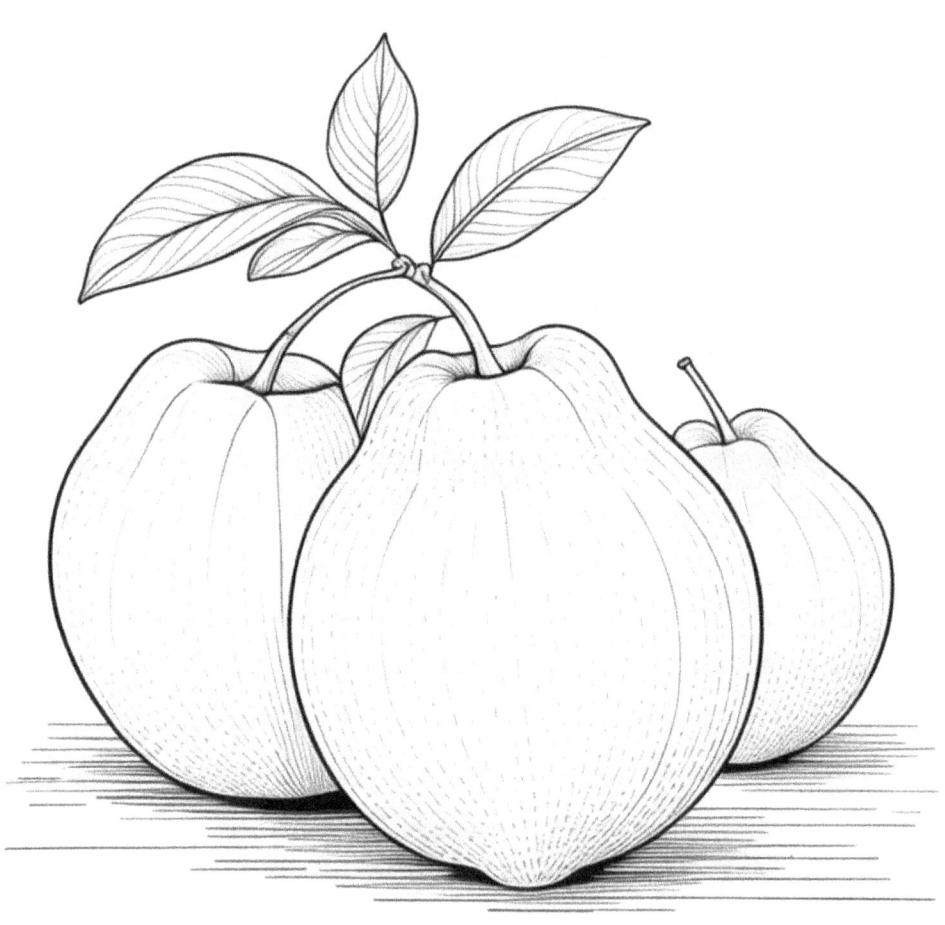

Quad bike

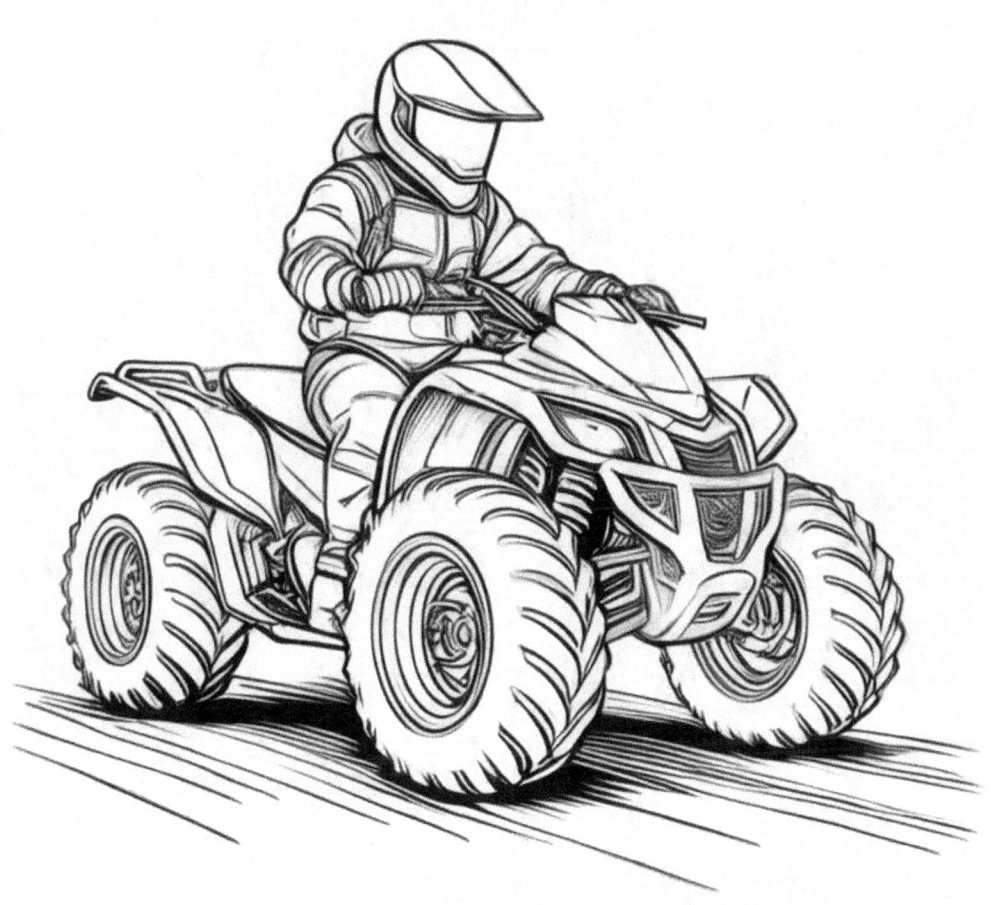

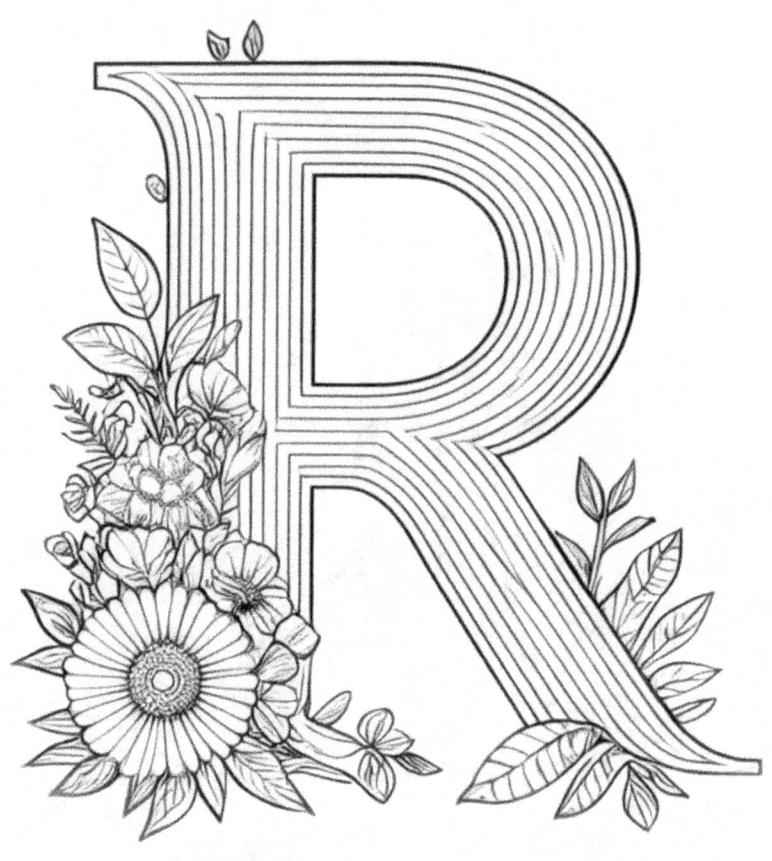

Rabbit

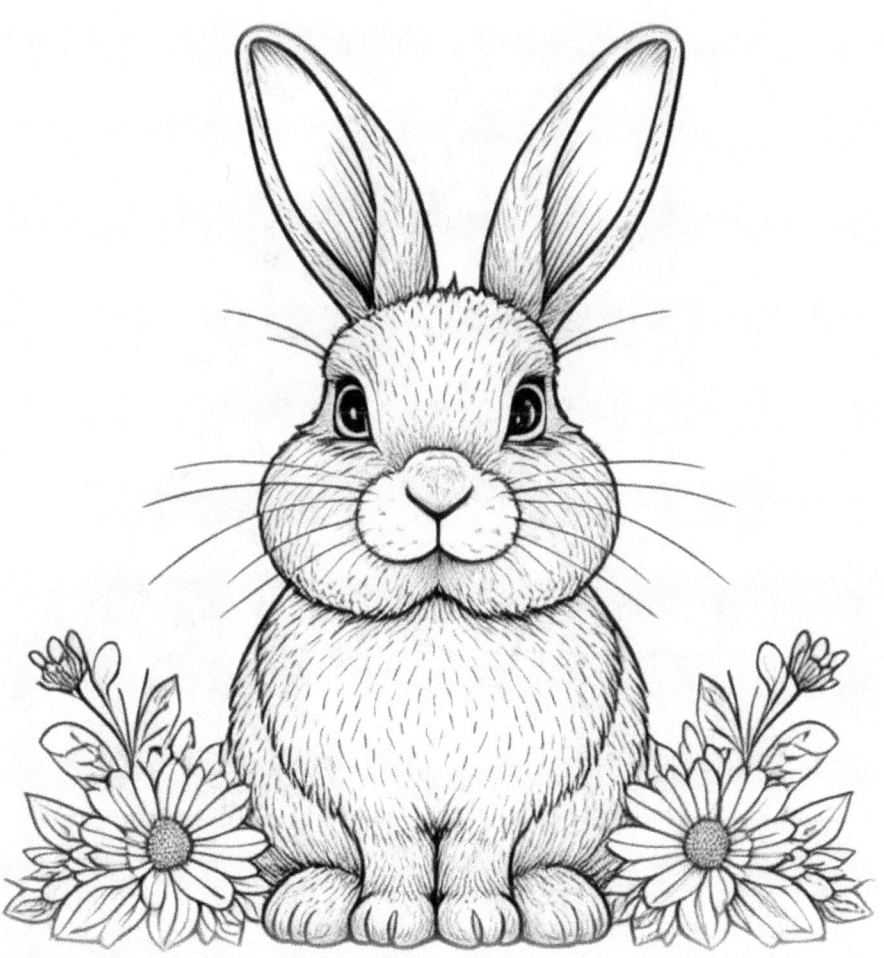

Raspberry

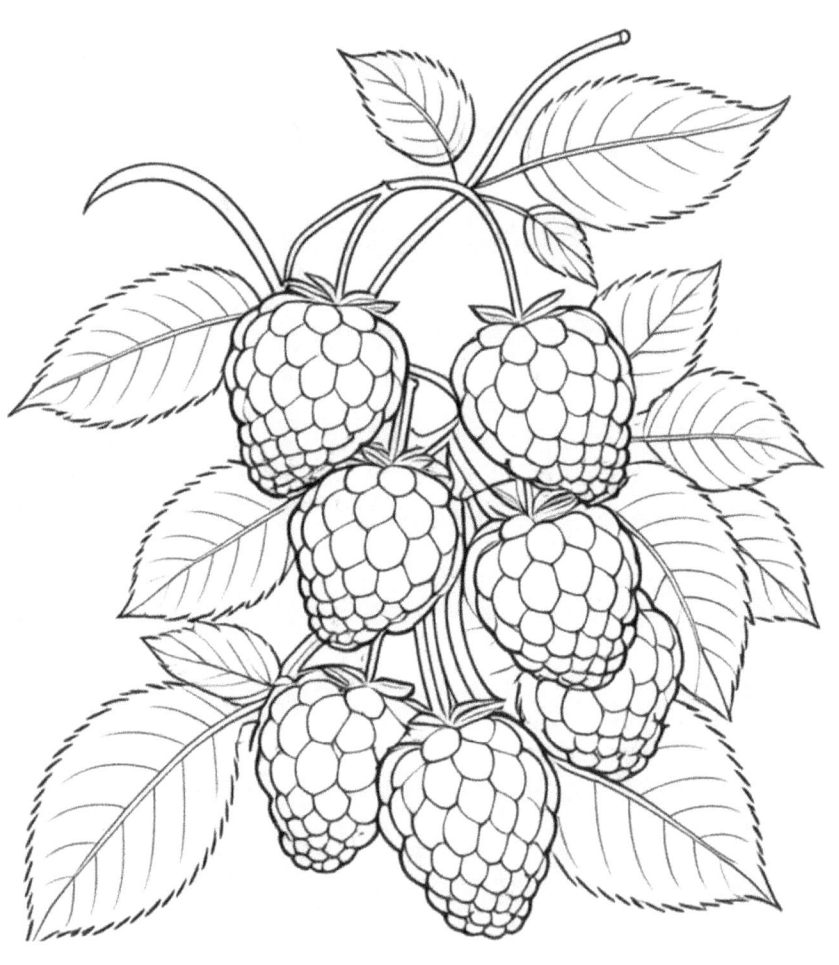

Rocket

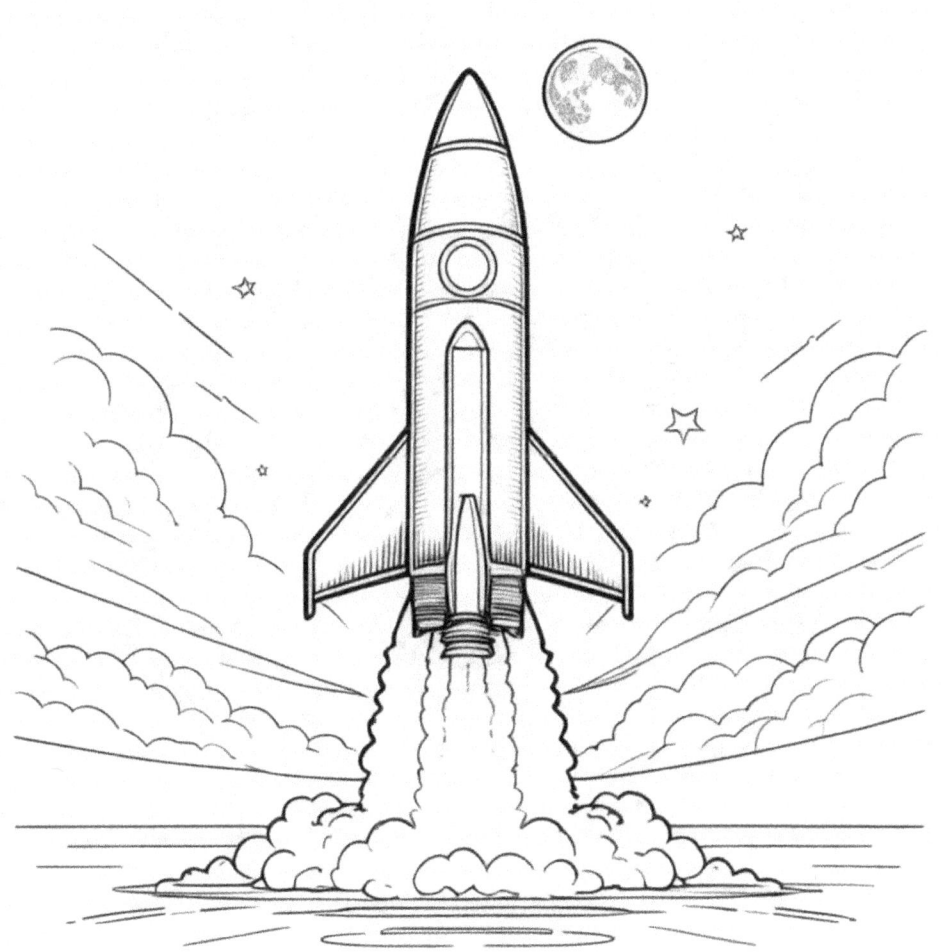

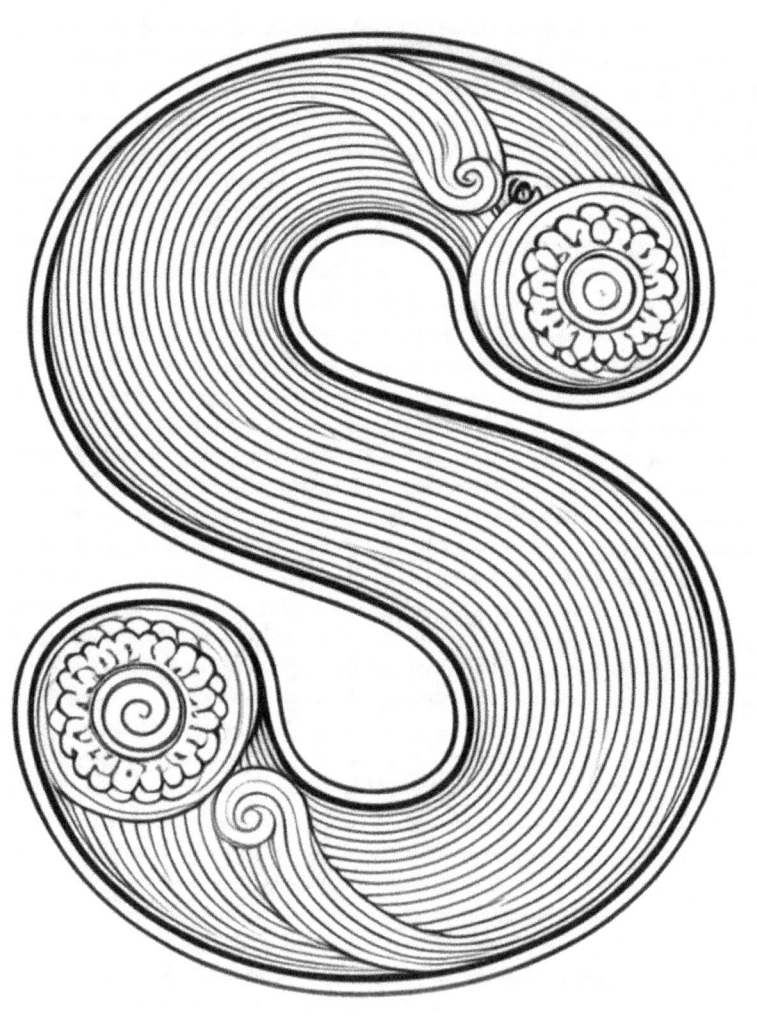

Squirrel

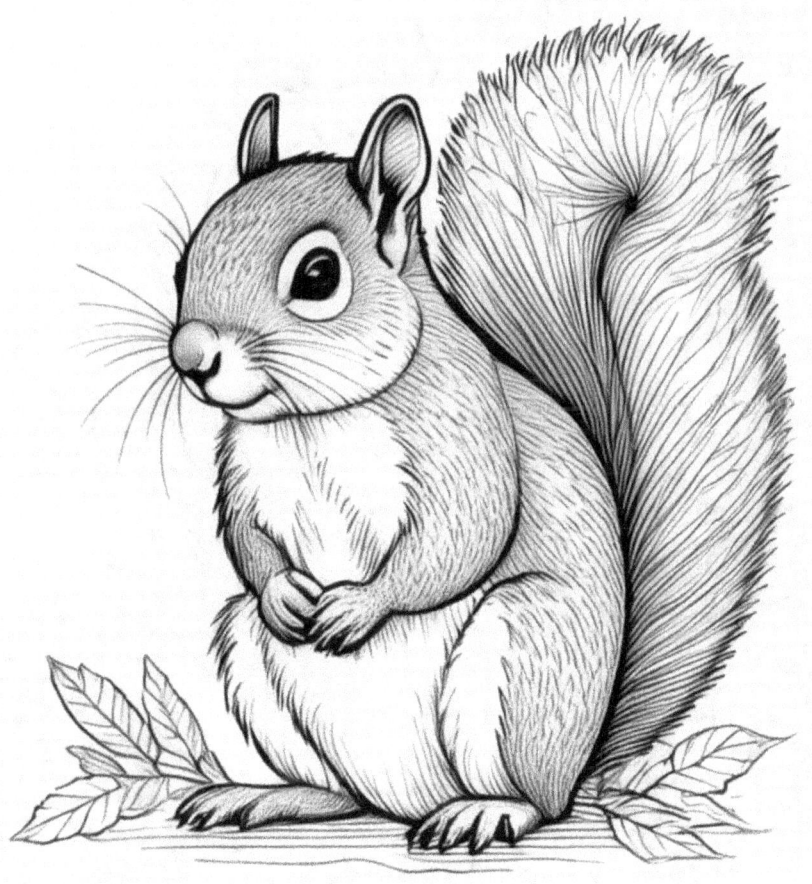

Strawberry

Scooter

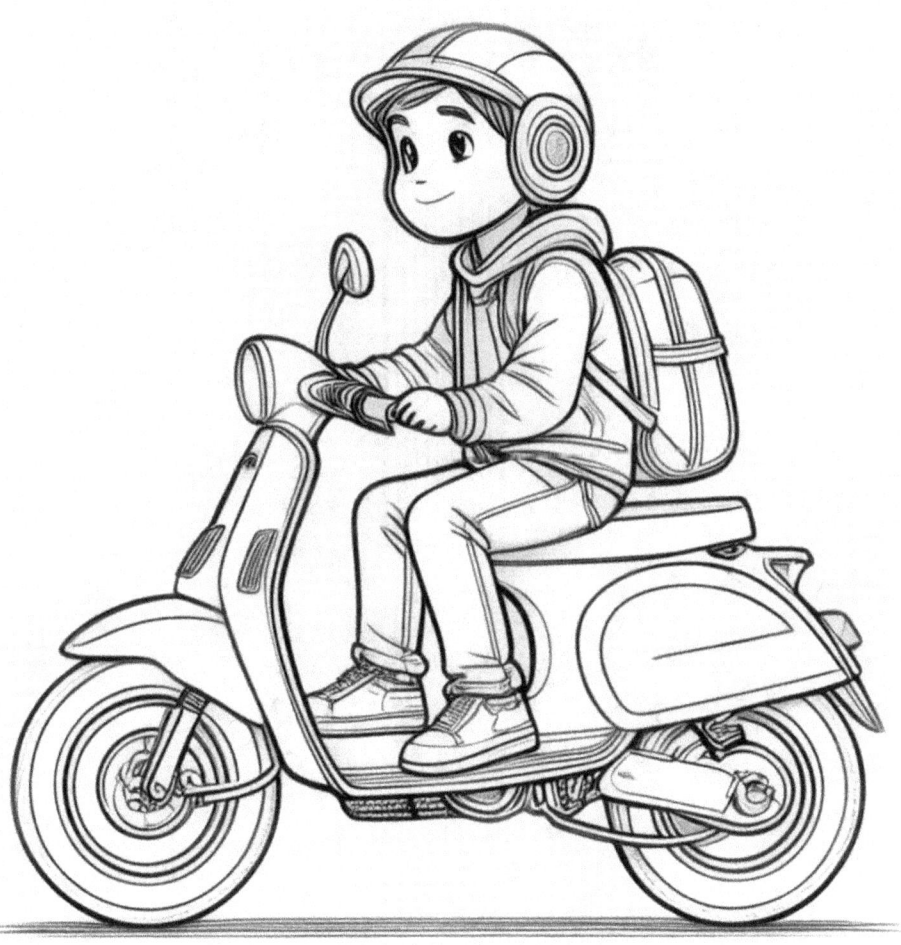

Tiger

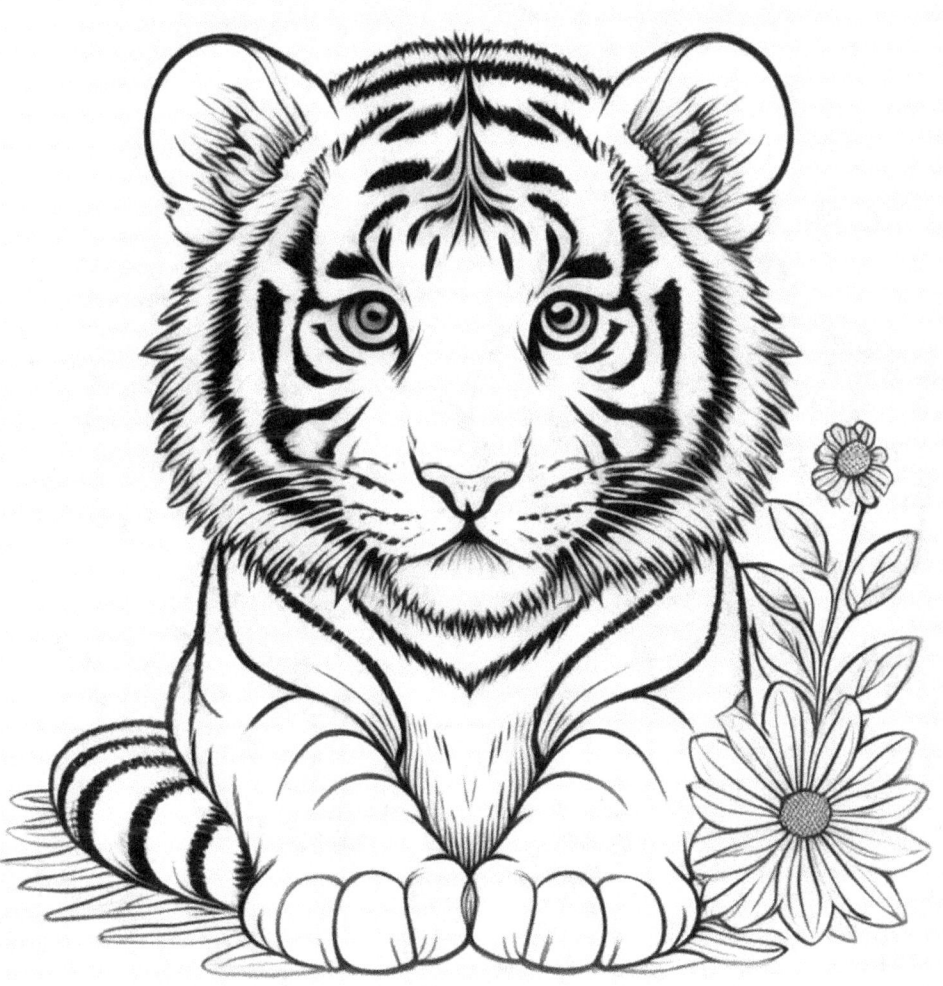

Tomato

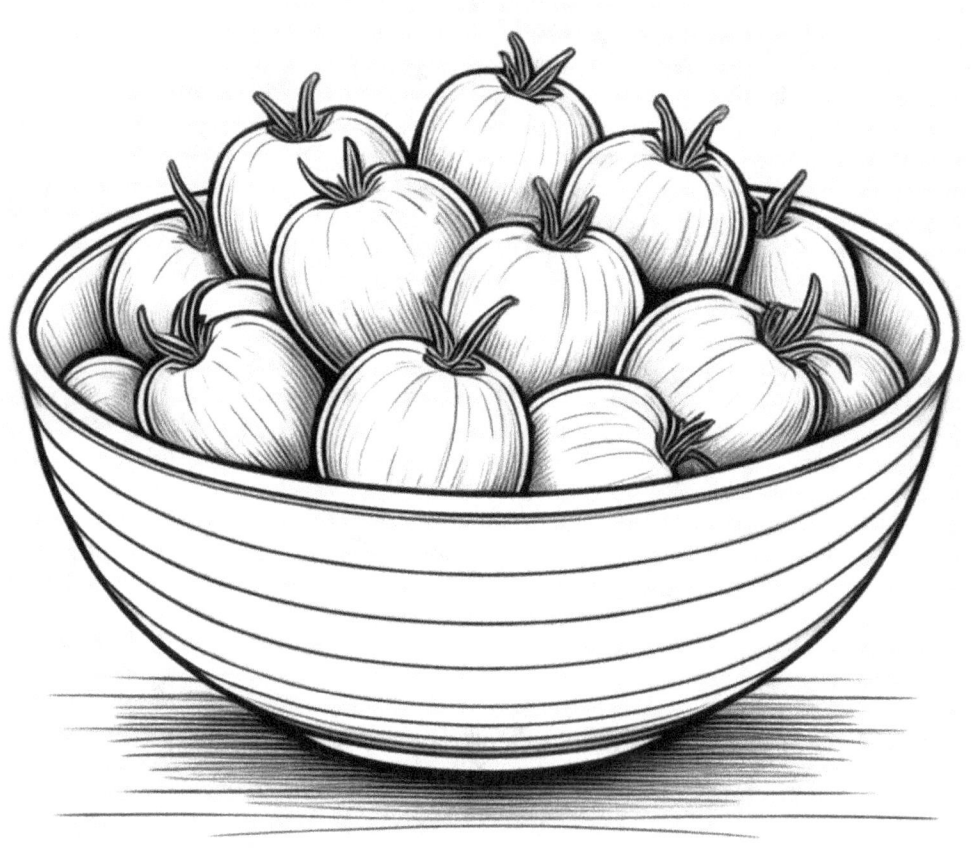

Train

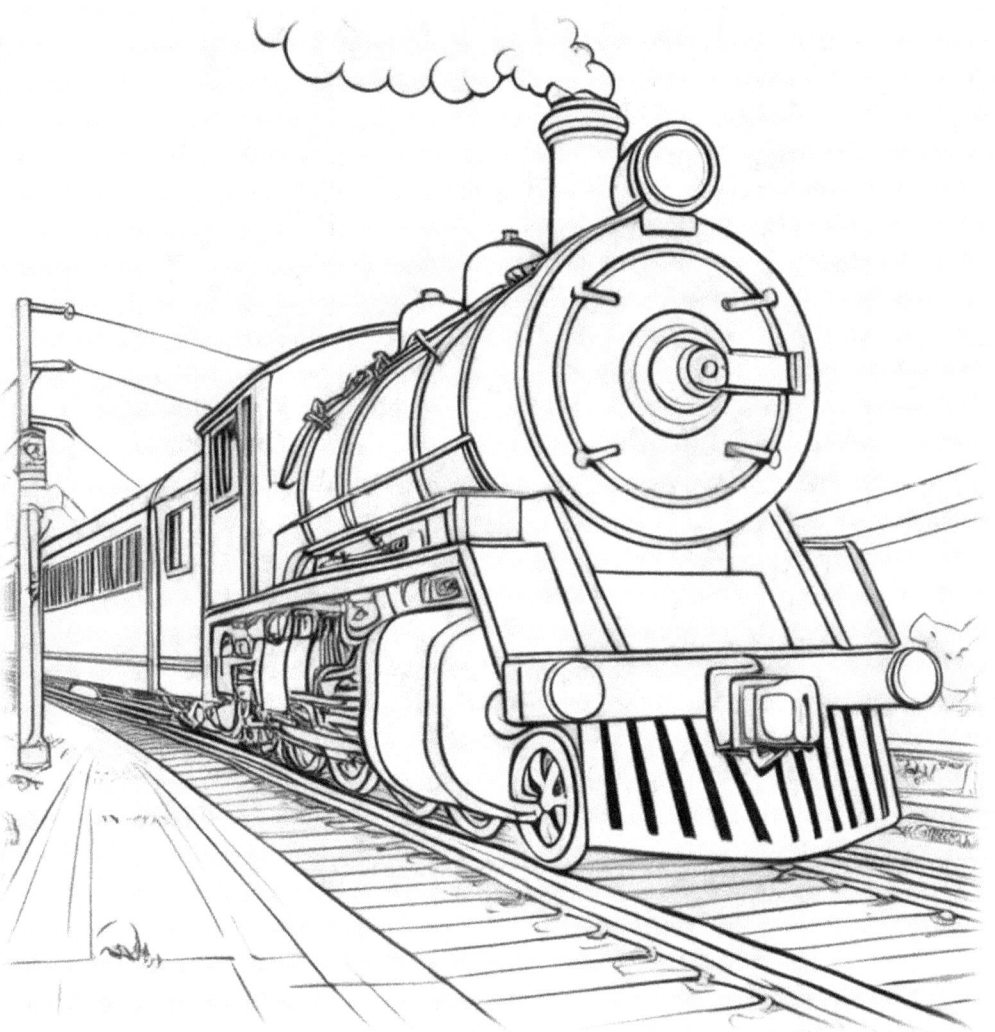

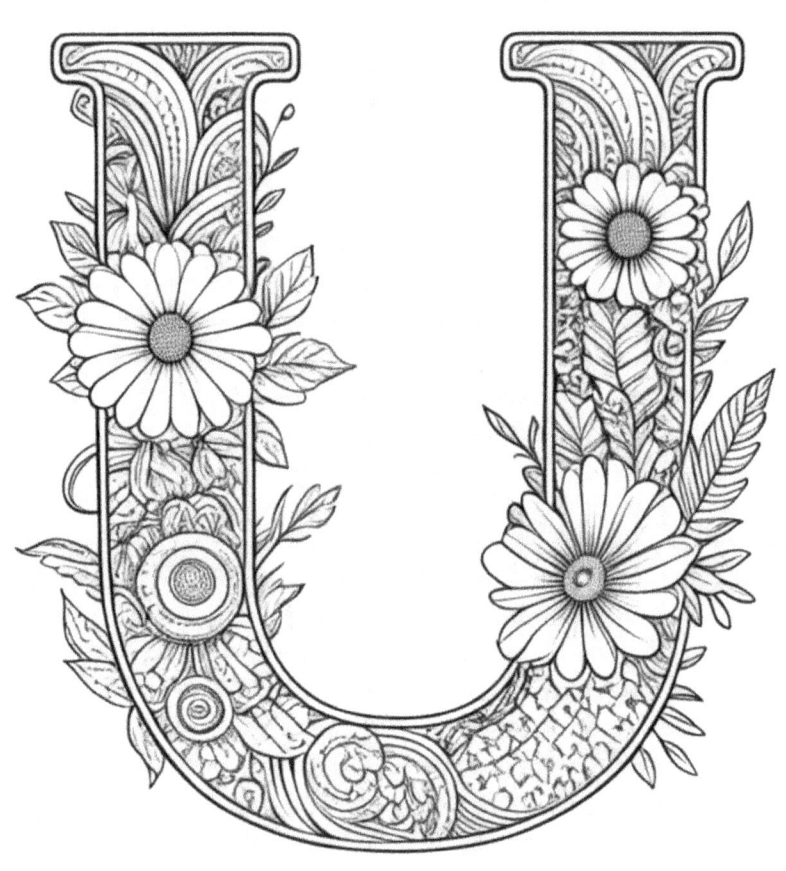

Umbrellabird

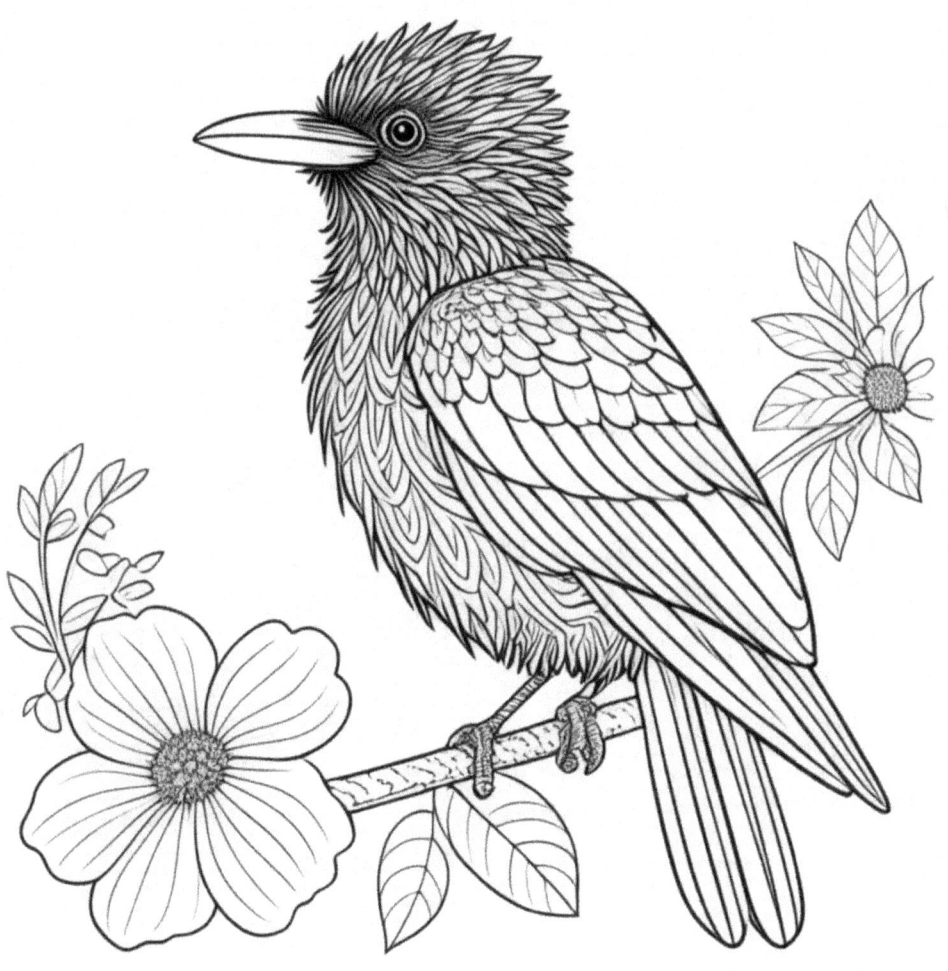

Ugli fruit

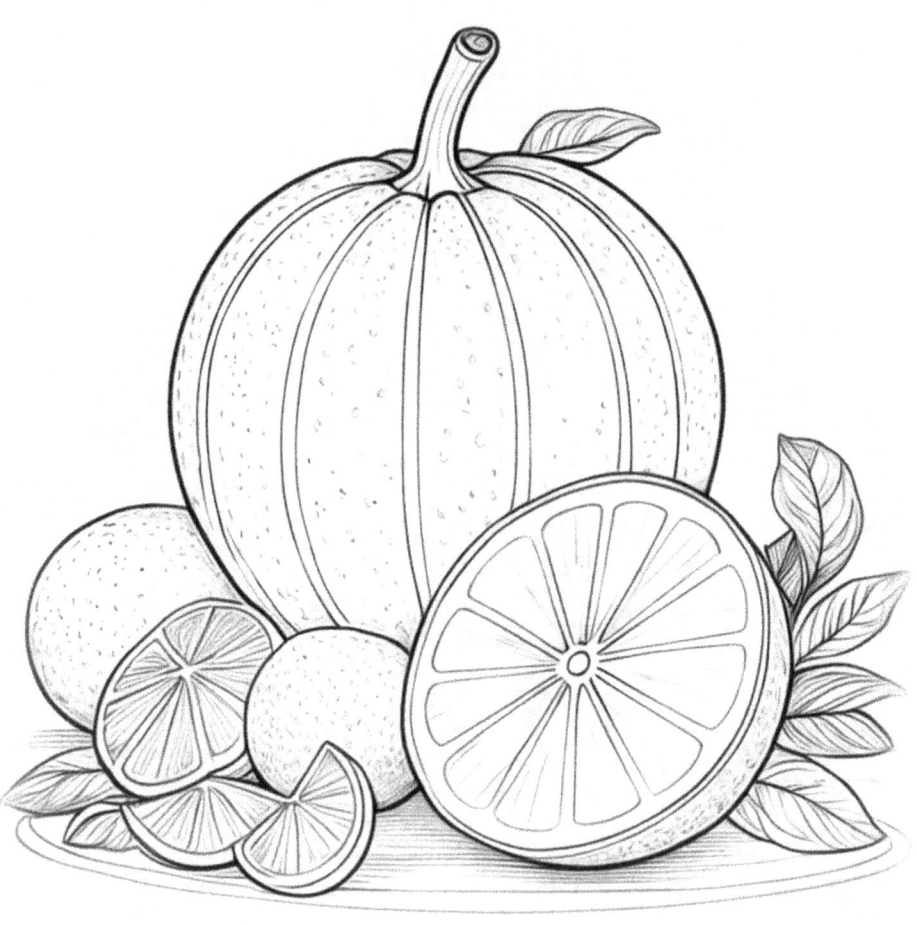

U-boat

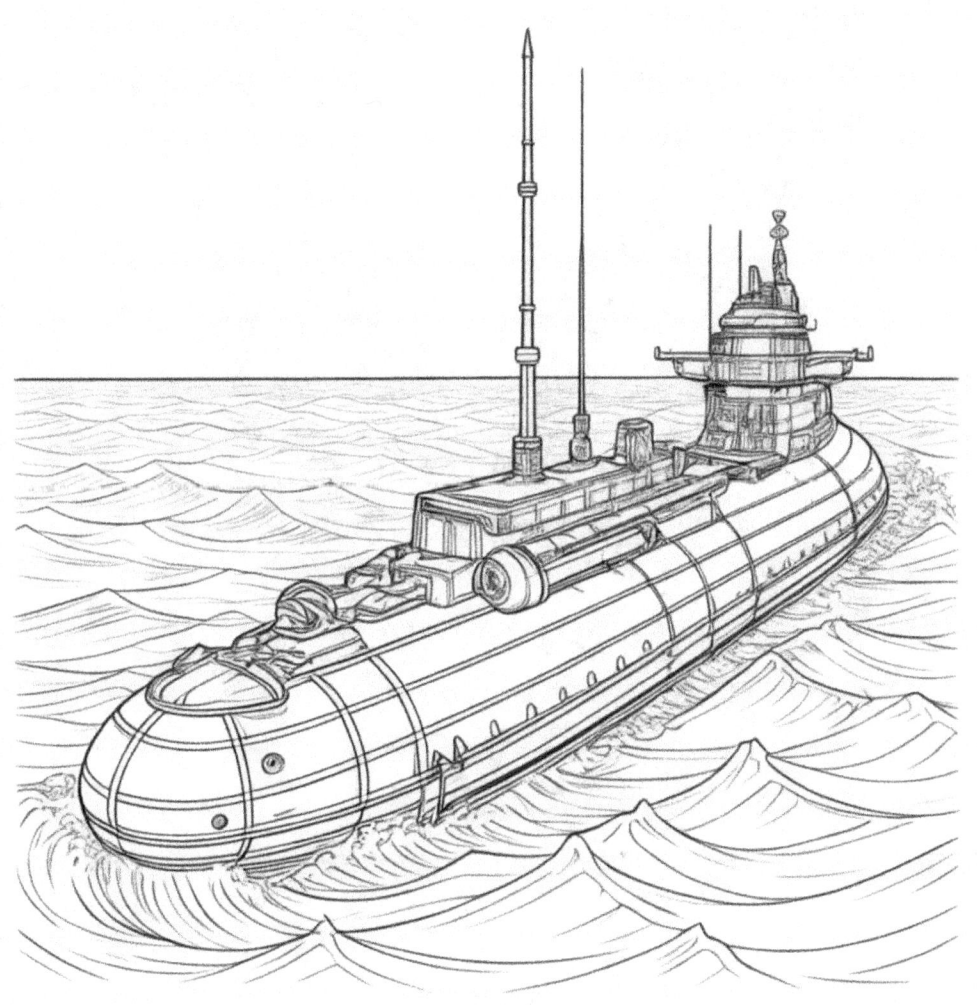

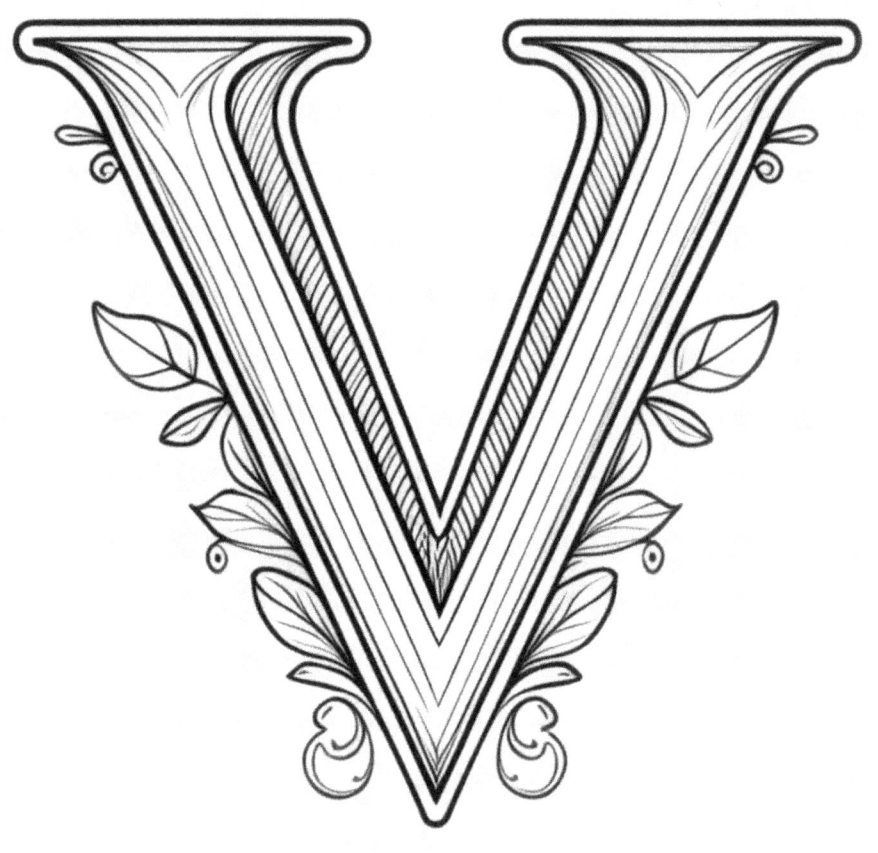

Vaquita

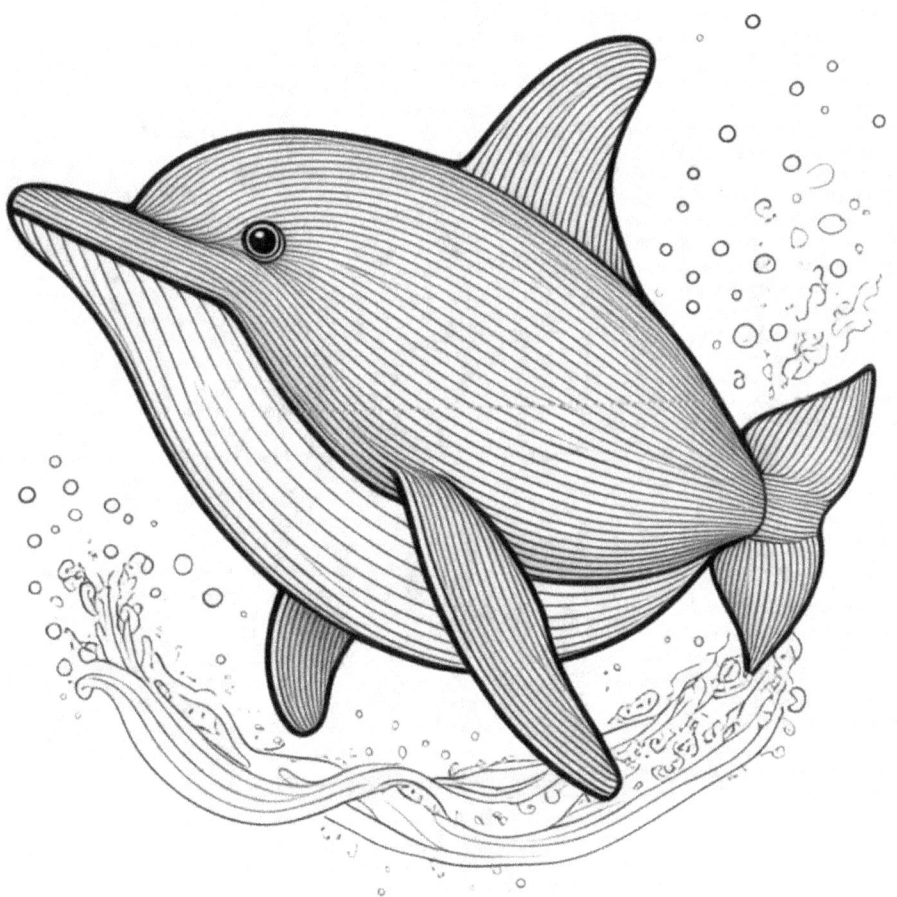

Violet

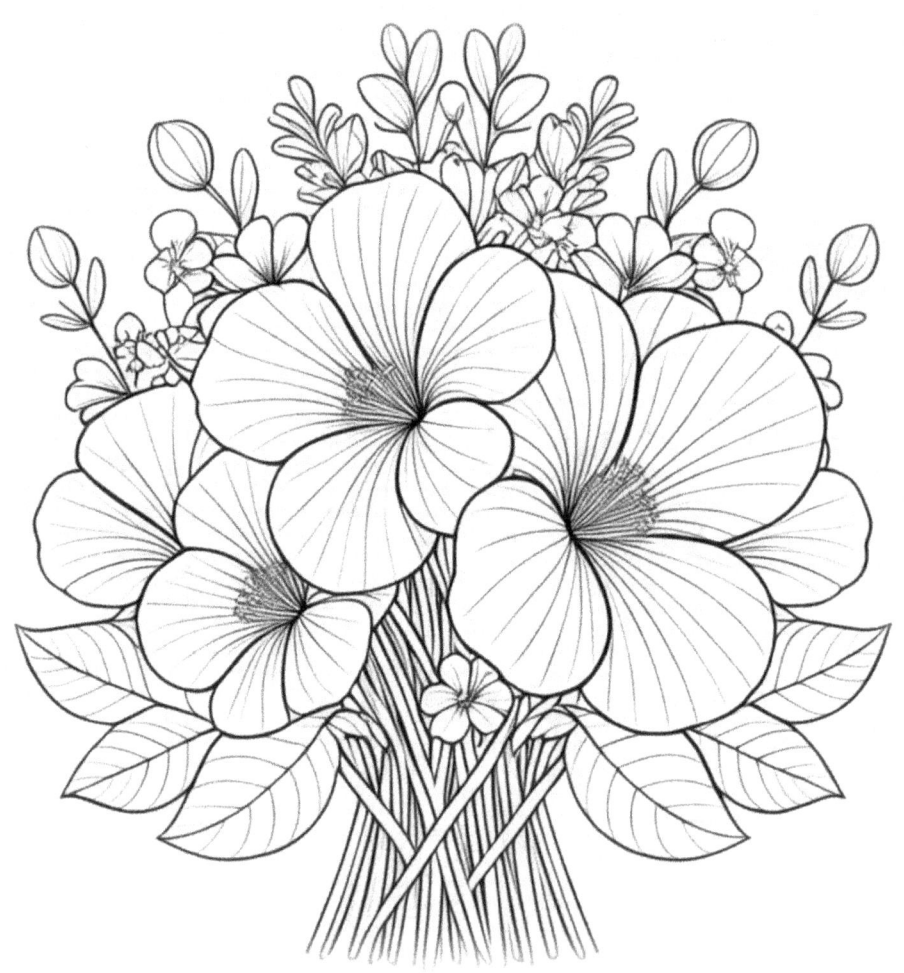

Van

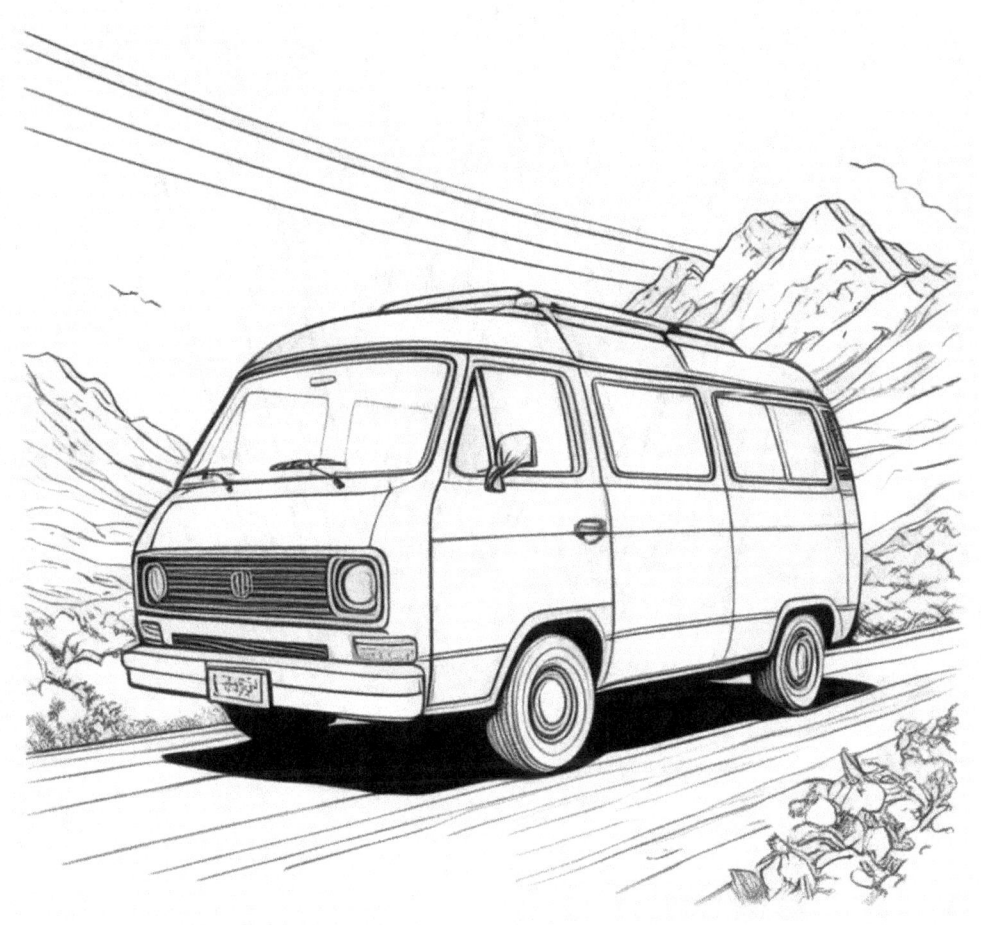

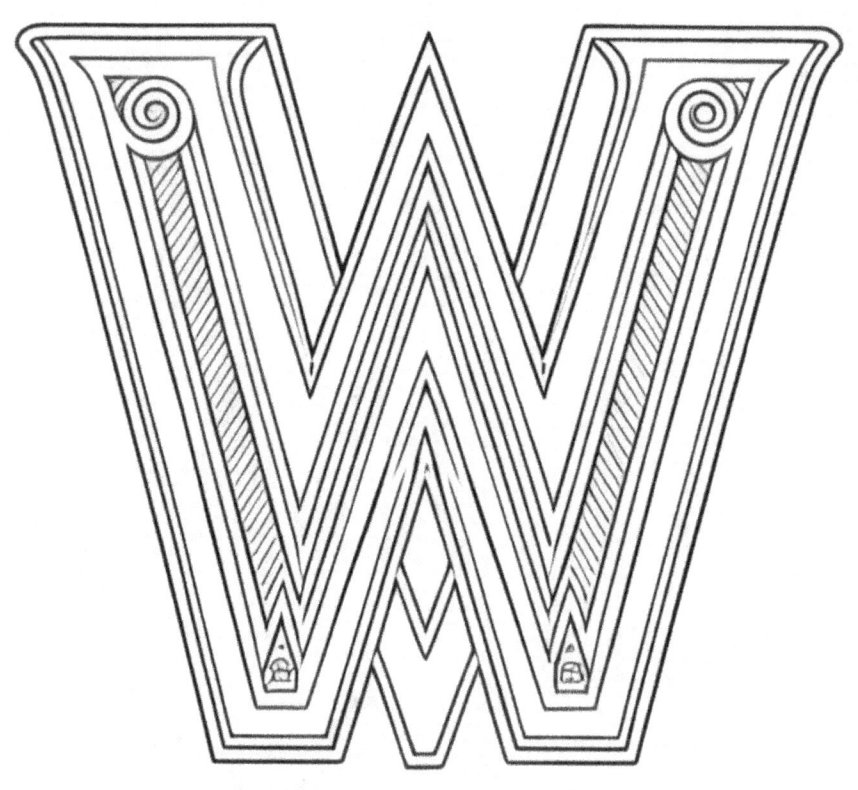

Wolf

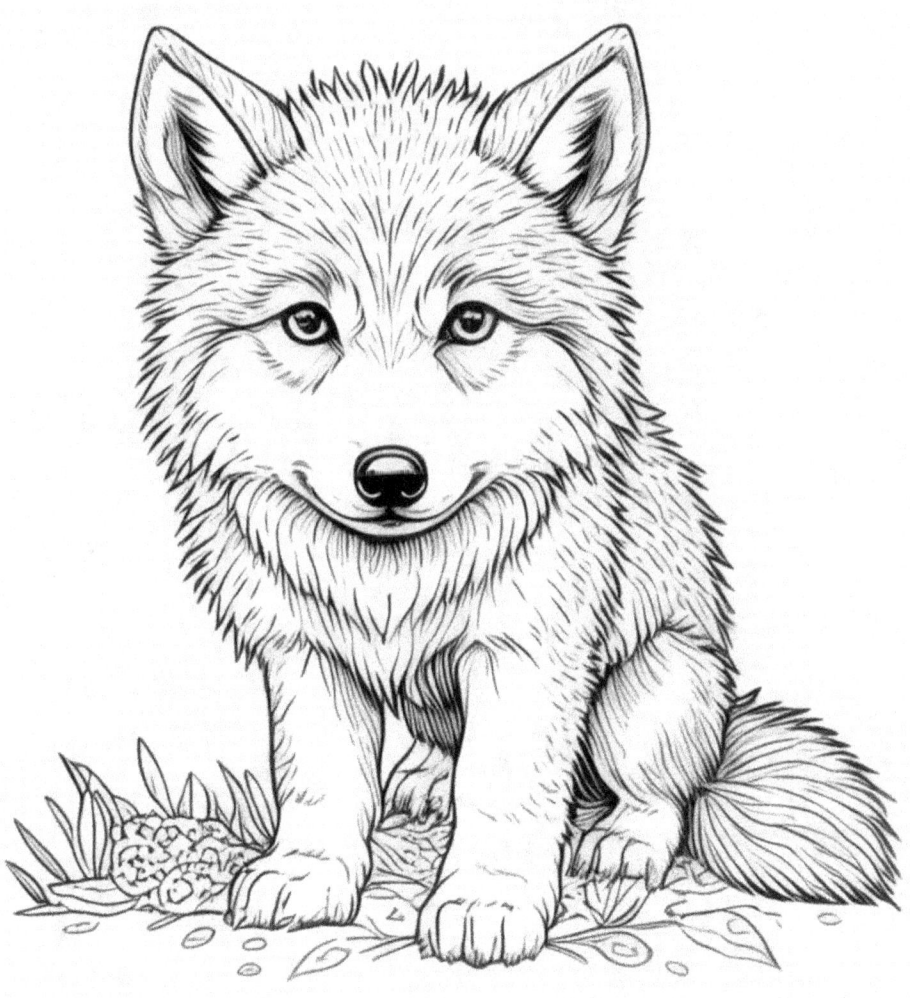

Watermelon

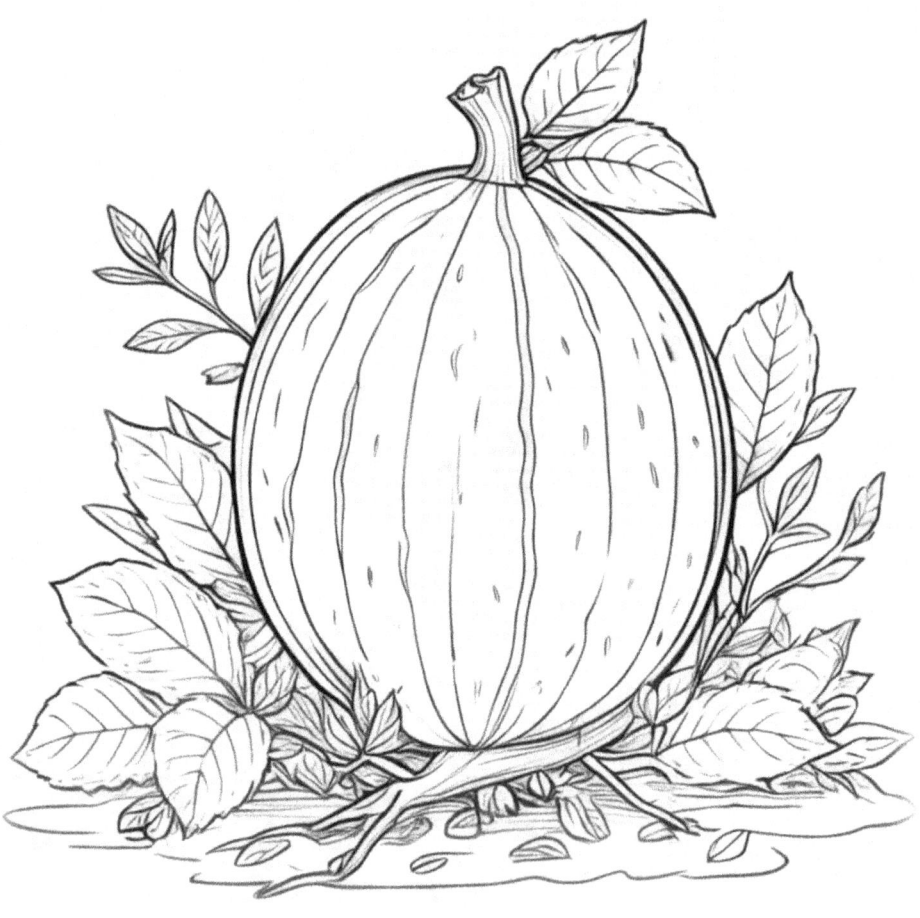

Wagon

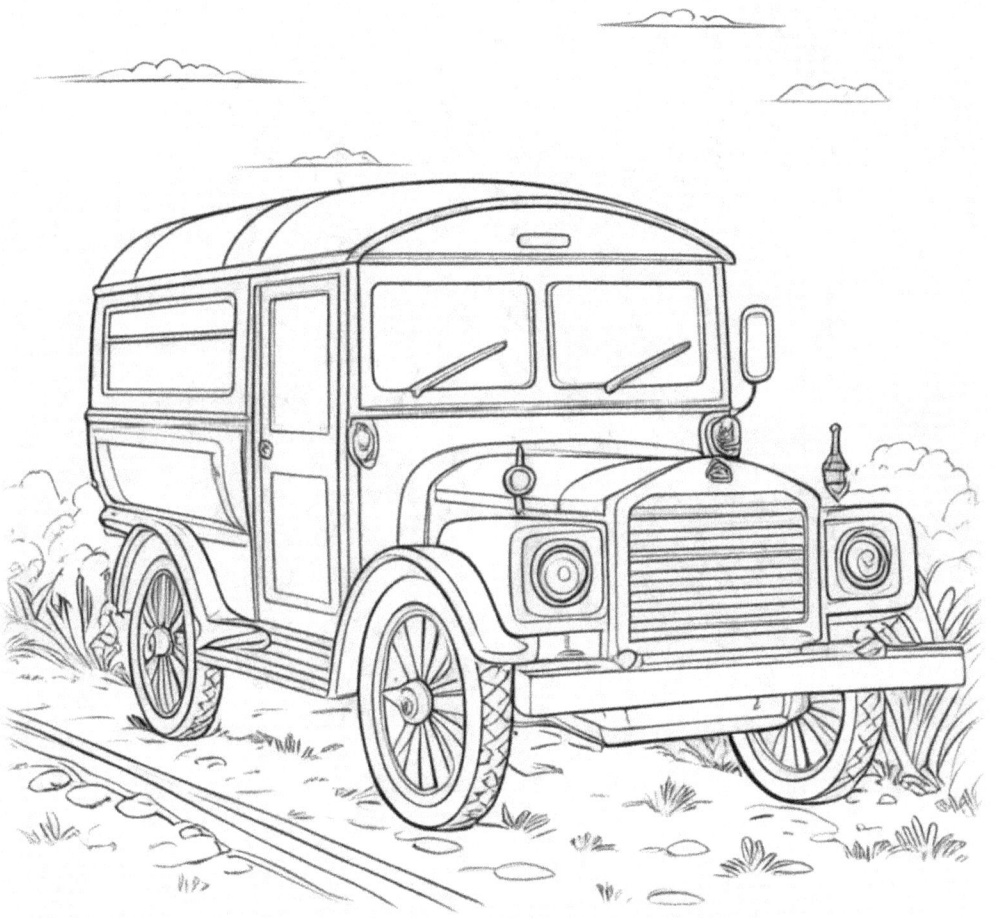

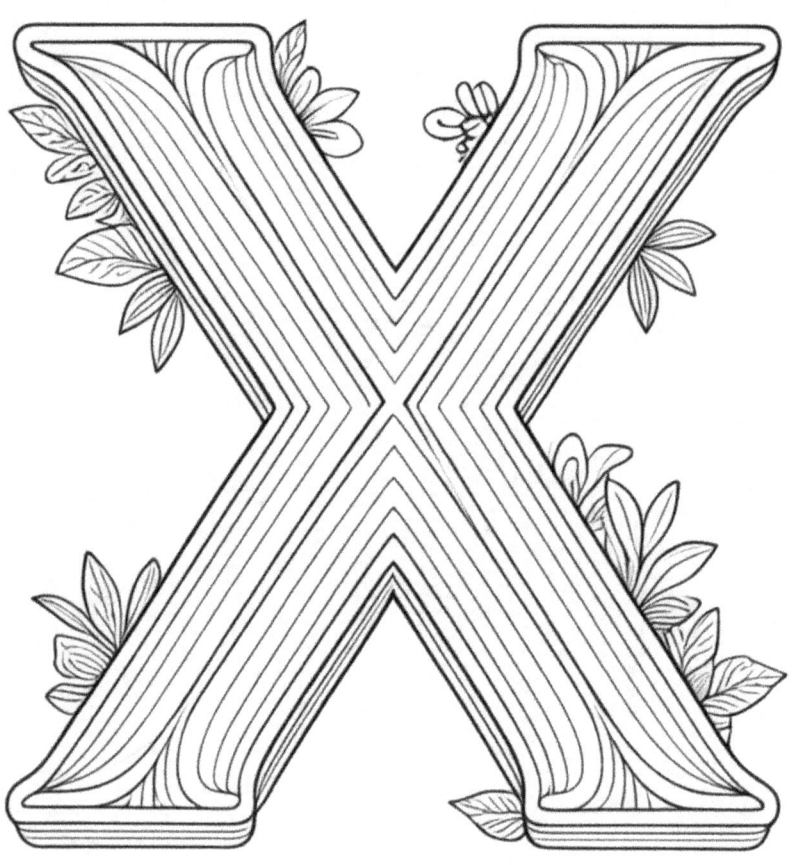

Xenopus

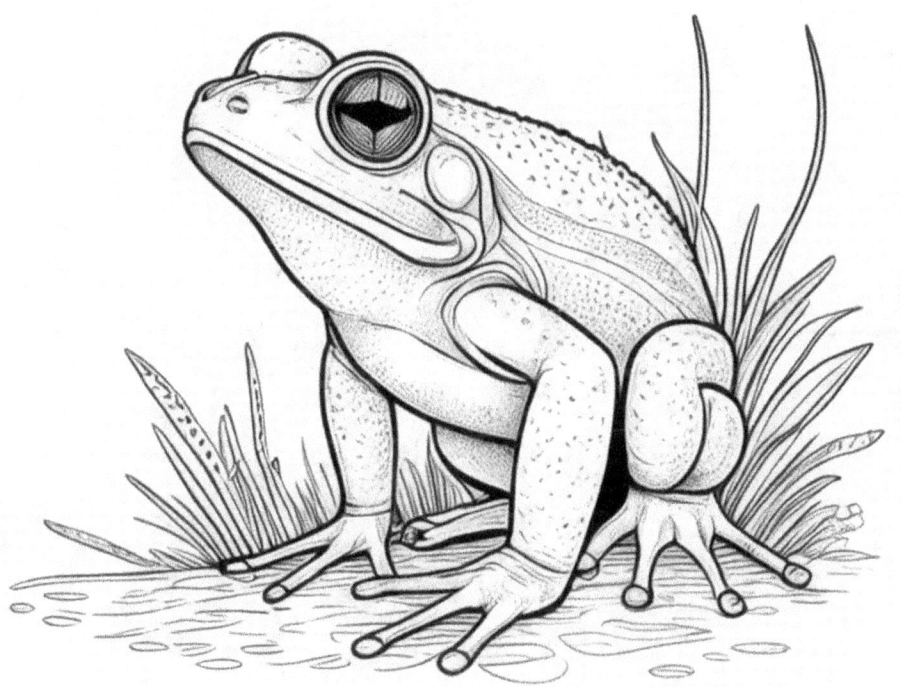

Xylocarp

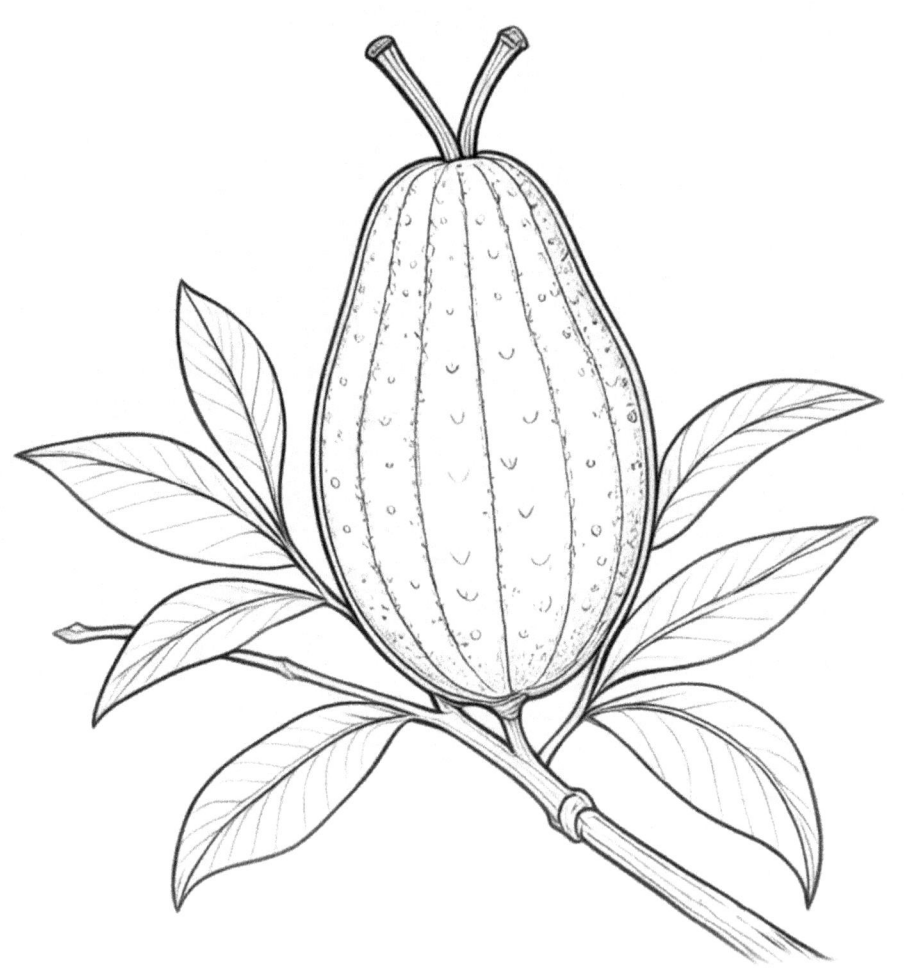

X15 Plane

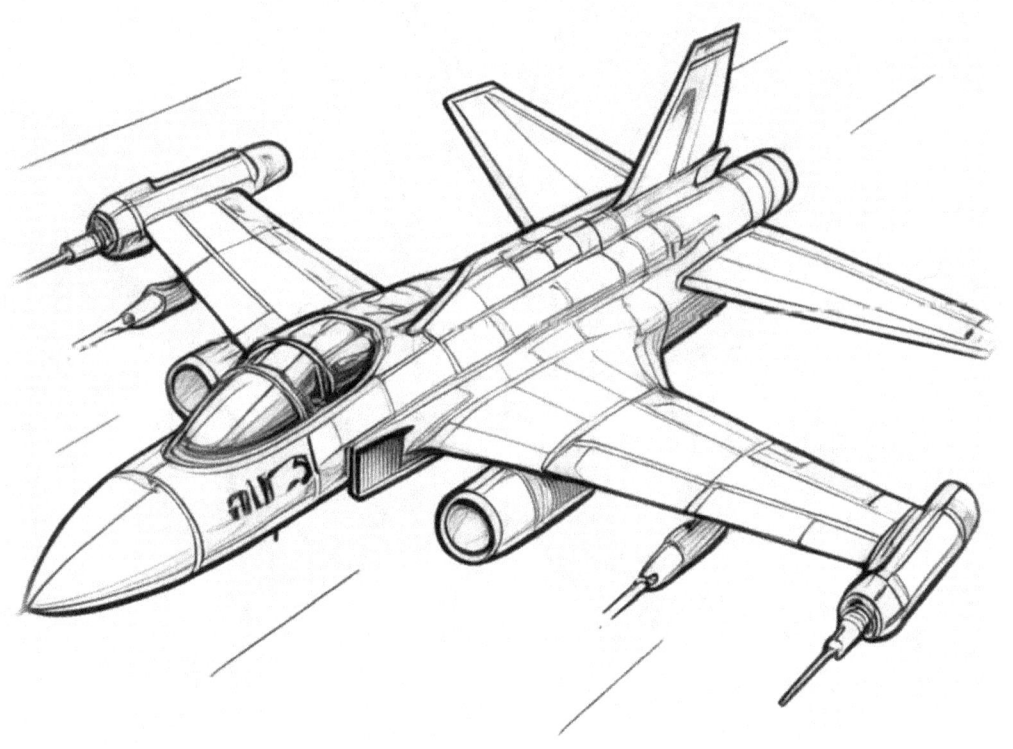

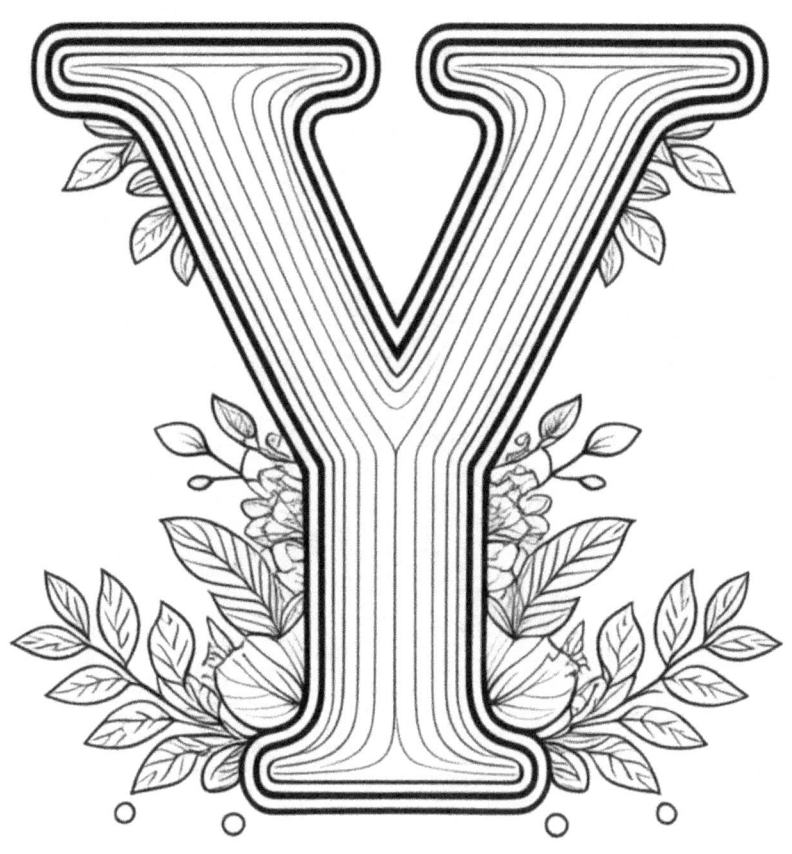

Yak

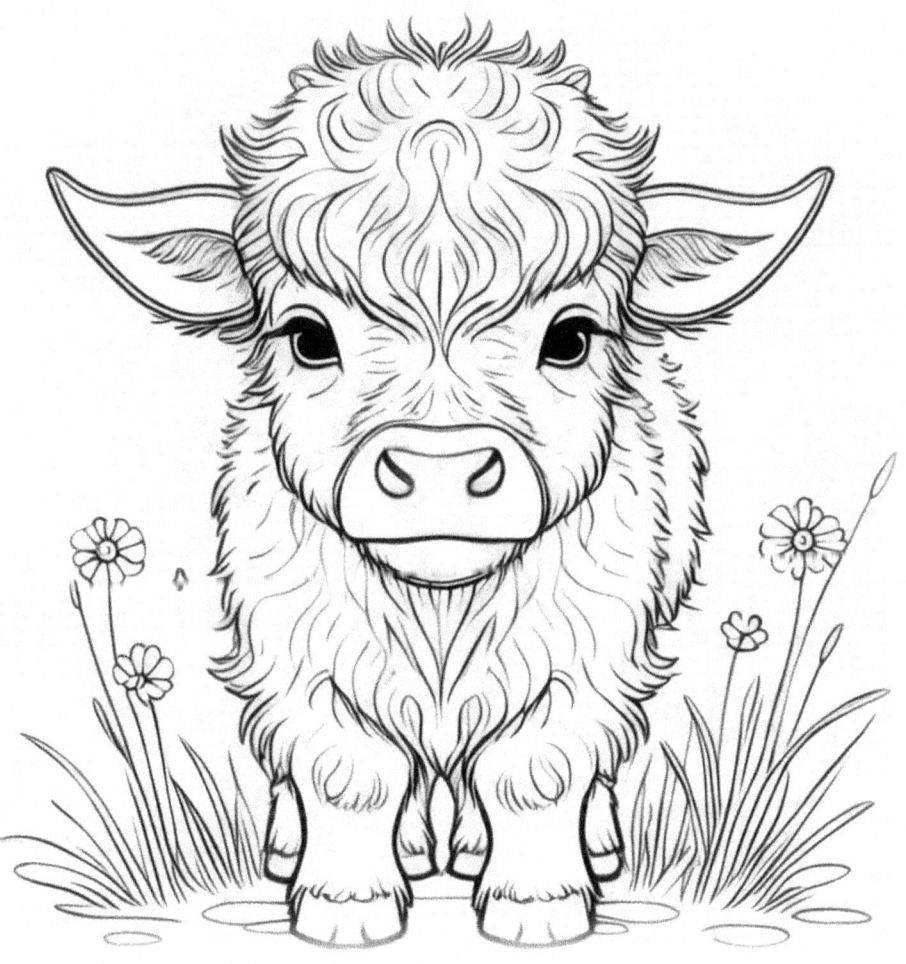

Ylang Ylang

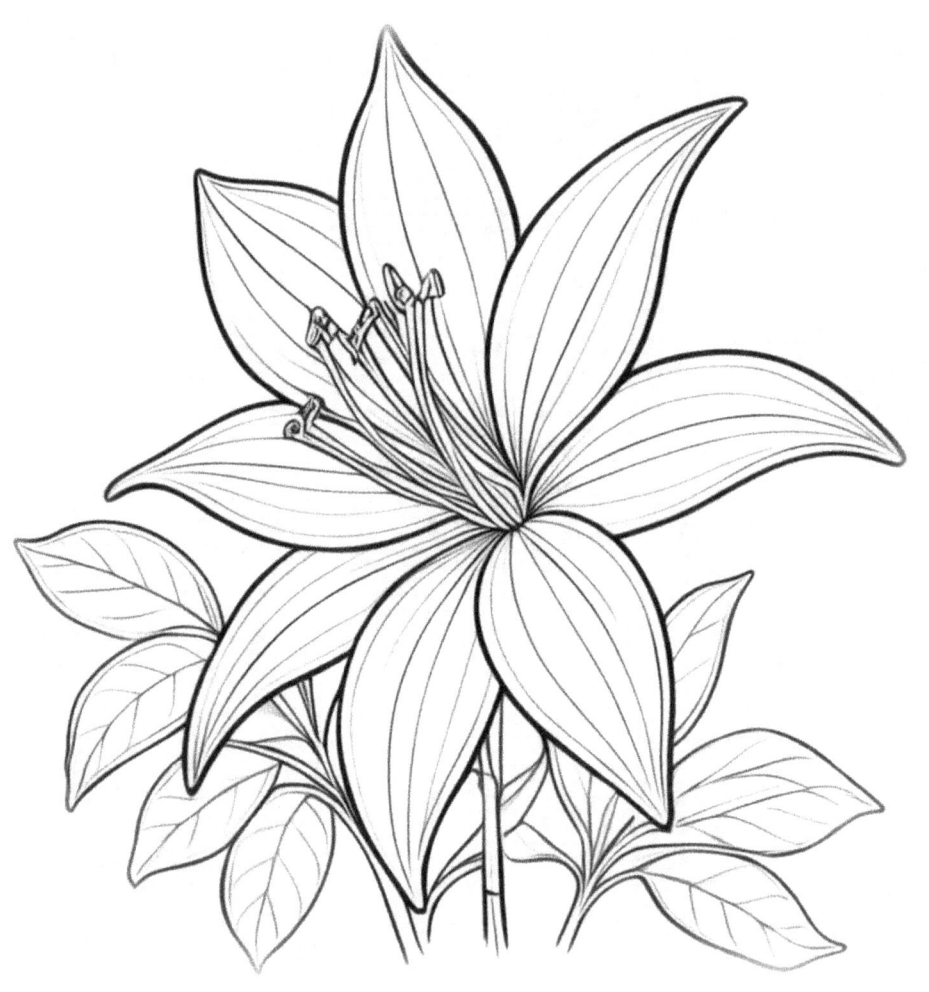

Yacht

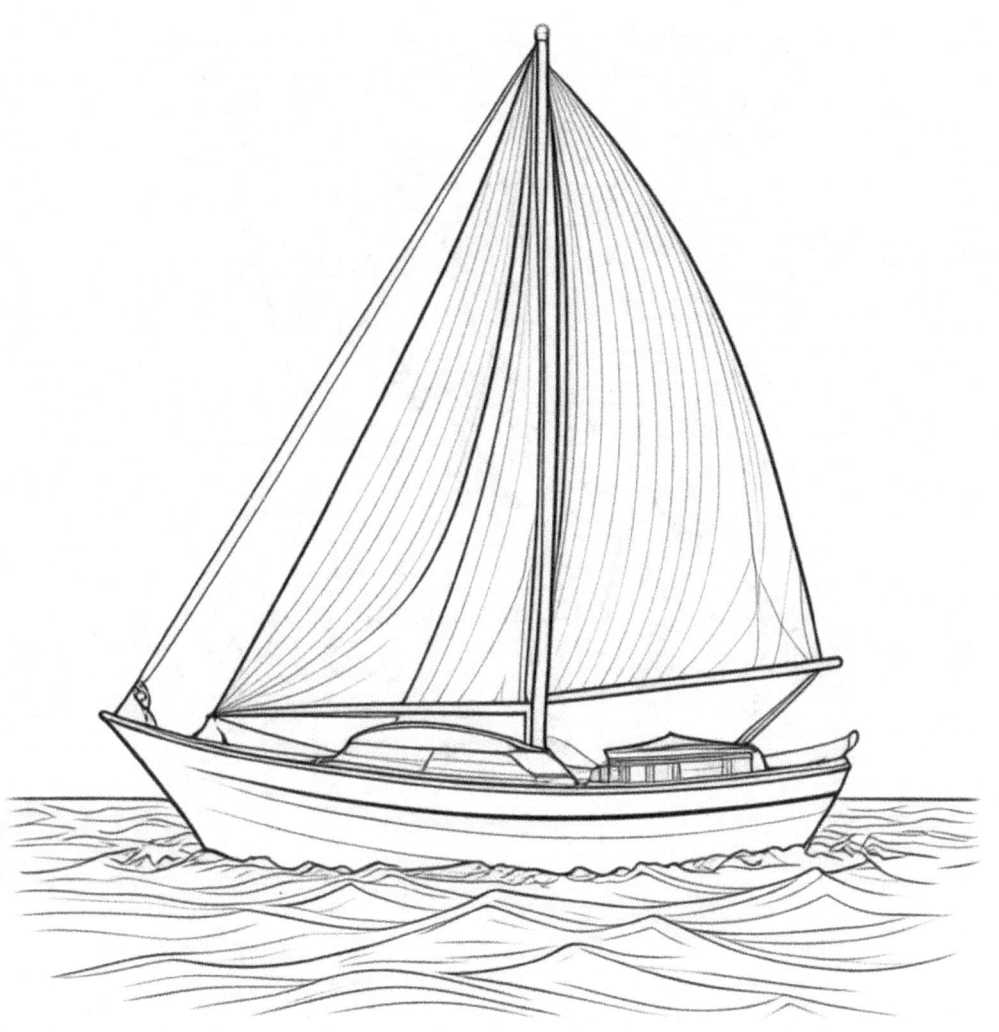

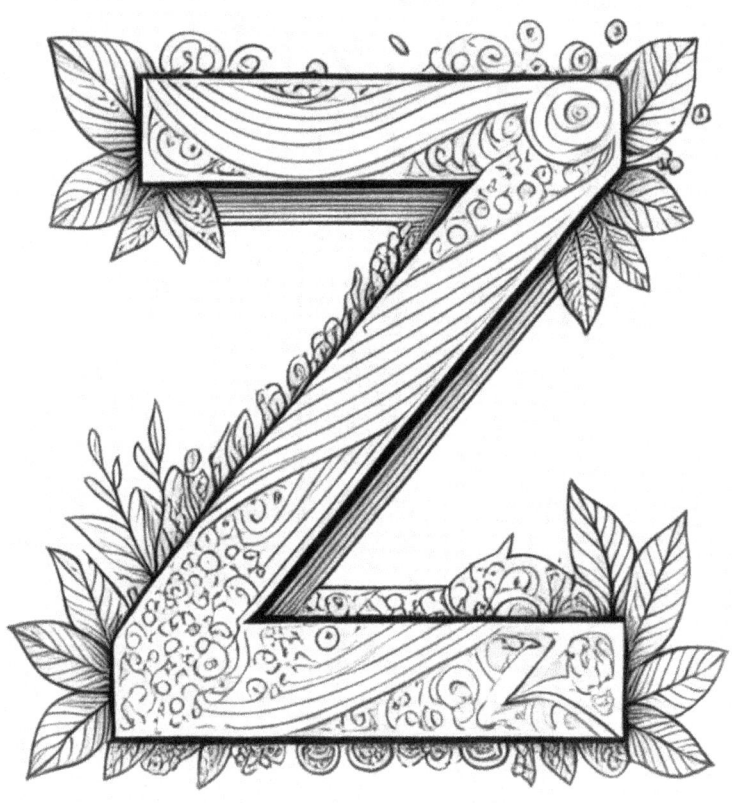

Zebra

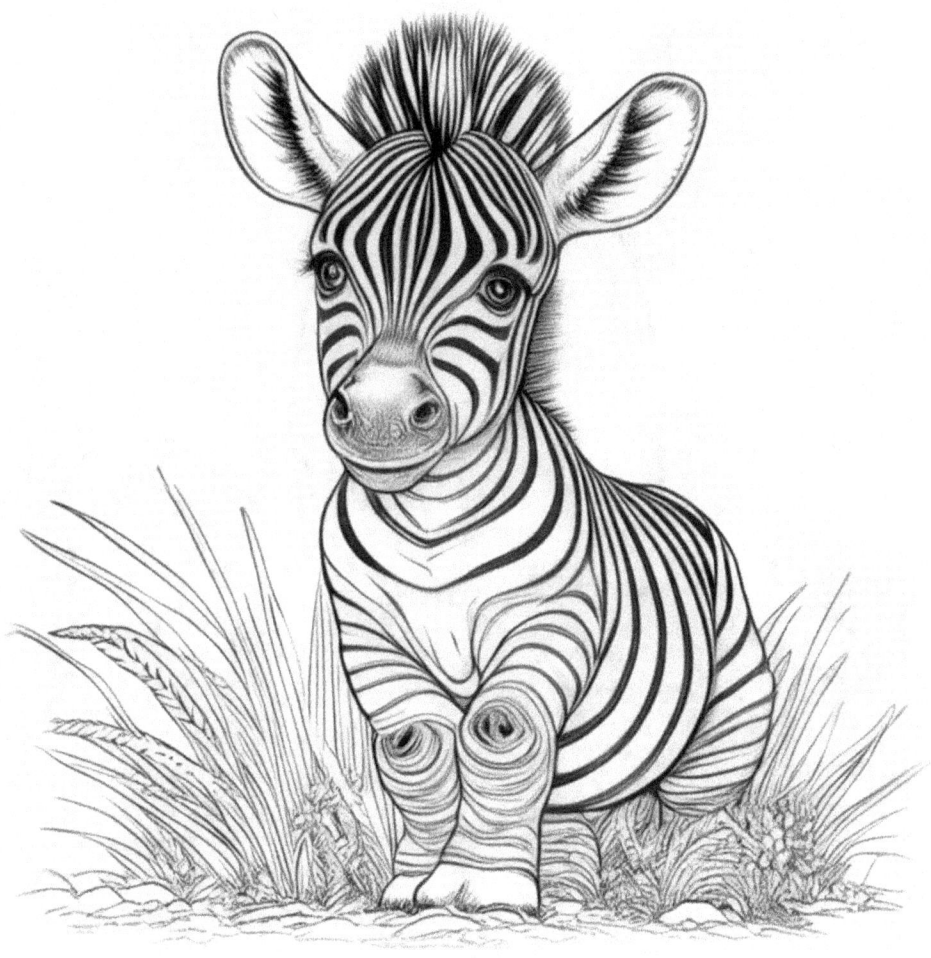

Zucchini

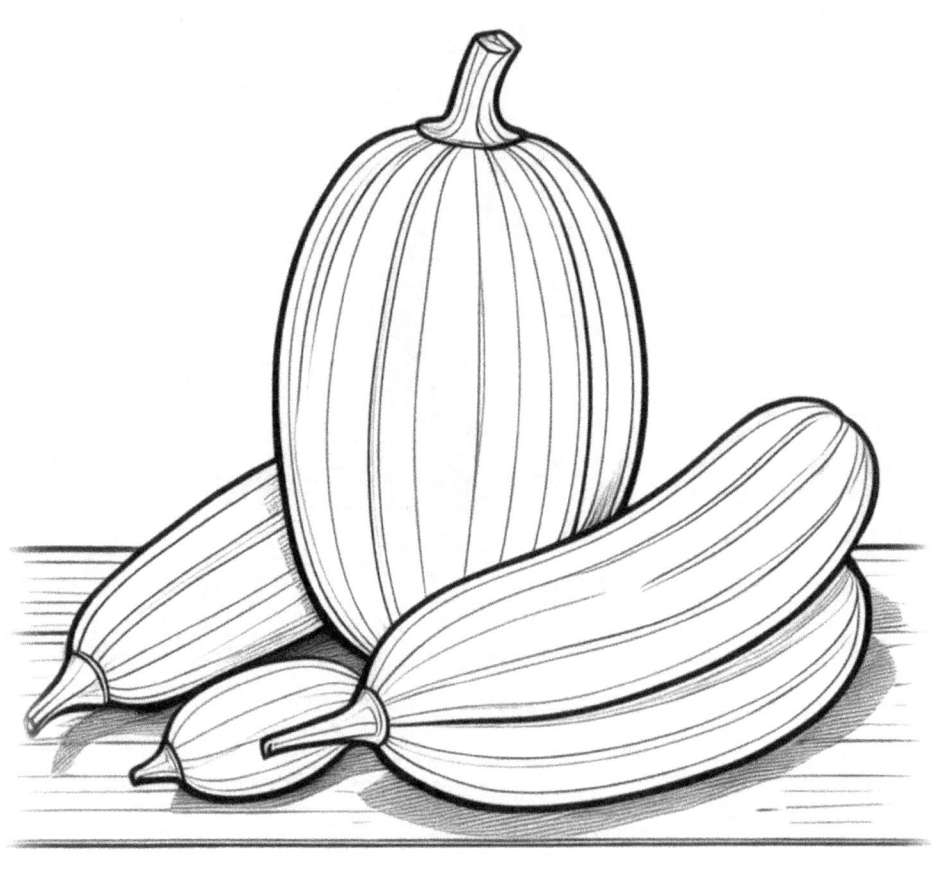

Zeppelin

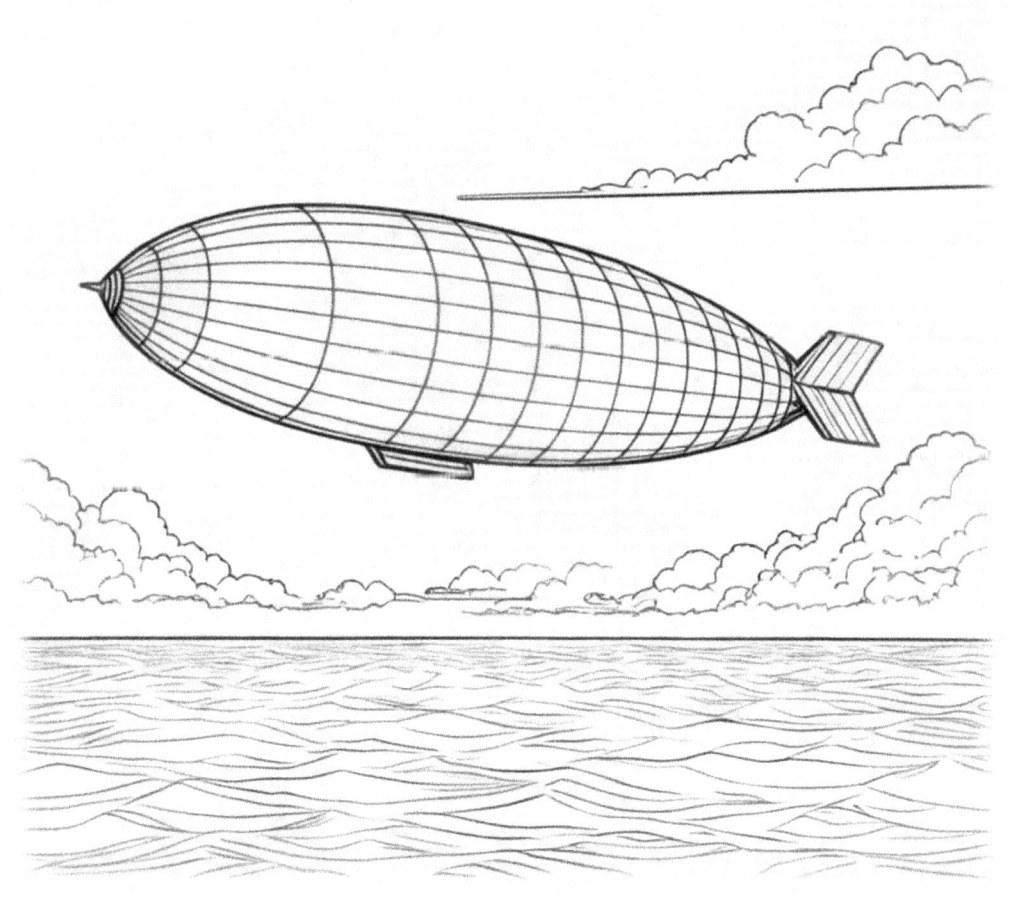

www.ingramcontent.com/pod-product-compliance
Lightning Source LLC
Chambersburg PA
CBHW050114230526
45470CB00004B/1829